To Emily –
May this book
richly bless you!
You are highly favored.

Lisa Jiménez

# SLAY
## THE
# DRAGON

## How to Get Out of Your Own Way and Get What You Want

# Praise for, *Slay the Dragon!*

"I love Lisa's new book. It will help you overcome your most formidable foe: yourself."

**- Randy Gage**
Author of the *New York Times* bestseller, *Risky Is the New Safe*


"Lisa Jimenez is uniquely qualified to help you slay the Dragons of Self-Sabotage.

I have championed her work for nearly twenty years. From her best-selling book, *Conquer Fear!* to the programs she has given at our public seminars, Lisa knows how to transform people and get results. Her next book, *Slay the Dragon* promises to be another major hit. If you want to break through the limitations that hold you back, read this book and get a copy for everyone on your team."

**- Bob Proctor**
Thought Leader on the Blockbuster movie, *The Secret* and author of the bestseller, *You Were Born Rich*


"With Lisa's new book, you'll get to face your Dragons head on. Through the story of her breakthrough, you'll be inspired to cause a breakthrough in your life, too. If you're ready to eradicate the limitations that keep you stuck, read my great friend Lisa's book."

**- Mark Victor Hansen**
Co-creator of the *Chicken Soup for the Soul* series as well as *The Miracles in You* and the world's best-selling author with over 500 million copies sold


"I know from first hand experience that Lisa knows how to take an ordinary person and transform them into extraordinary. She is especially gifted in helping you breakthrough the limitations that hold you back! Her book, *Slay the Dragon* is a must read for anyone in pursuit of their highest calling."

**- Carla Burns**
Ambassador Diamond, It Works Global and author of, *Claim your Power* and *As it is Written, So it is!*

"The biggest challenges we ever face are the ones we create for ourselves. This book will show you how to slay those dragons of self-sabotage."

**-Art Jonak**
MastermindEvent founder, Entrepreneur and World-Class Networker

"Slay the Dragon is easy to read and filled with Lisa's heart-felt story. It will help you identify what limiting programs are keeping you from success. Through practical exercises and examples, you'll slay those dragons once and for all!"

**-Hilde Rismyhr Saele**
Co-Founder and Elite President at Zinzino

"A couple of our top leaders and I participated in one of Lisa's *Rich Life Mastermind Retreats*. That experience was a defining year that helped accelerate the growth in our organization globally. When I heard about her new book, *Slay the Dragon* I had to read it and share it with our team members. This book will help you identify and break through your limitations and build beyond them."

**- Tammy Sellars-Gingras**
Max International Crown Diamond Global Leader

"Sometimes a message comes along in a whole new way that it is a sudden mental two-by-four to your mind. This happened with me with Lisa Jimenez's newest book. Wow! Lisa has put into words how she sees overcoming adversity in a way that is fresh and brilliant. To say that parts of this work is profound is an understatement. I highly recommend anyone that wants to CRUSH every barrier in their life to read this book."

- **Dr. Doug Firebaugh**
CEO DFTI and host of "The Millionaire Road" - National Radio Show

"Add, *Slay the Dragon* to your library of personal development classics; which I'm sure needs more books authored by women. All of us are called to step into our power and Lisa Jimenez continues to lead the way."

- **Dr. Josephine Gross**
Editor-in-Chief of *Networking Times*

"This book is a well crafted work that clearly demonstrates the self-imposed barriers that once addressed will clear the path for success in all areas of your life."

- **Jim Lutes**
Author of Life Masterpiece

"Lisa Jimenez is uniquely qualified to help you slay the Dragons of Self-Sabotage. With a background in psychology, Lisa understands people. Her life is proof that what she teaches actually works. In a world where too many self help books are written by people who haven't achieved any measurable success; Lisa's results put this book at the top of my books to read and recommend."

- **Dana Collins**
National Executive Vice President at Arbonne International

"Lisa dug deep with this one. She shares the raw struggles and breakthroughs she had with her own Dragons, and gives us a process to follow that gets results."
**- Deborah Crowe**
Work Life Balance Specialist and co-Author of *The Change 5*


"*Slay the Dragon* will encourage and inspire you. Lisa Jimenez has written a heart felt book based on her experiences, what she learned and what you can learn to stop self-sabotage. Read it to get valuable tools to slay the Dragons that keep you from achieving your potential."
**- Mark Sanborn**
Author of *The Fred Factor* and *You Don't Need a Title to be a Leader*


"I've been speaking, consulting and writing on what it takes to reach for new possibilities for a very long time. Lisa's message cut through what I've known forever, causing me to hear it freshly and vibrantly. There's a lot of blood, sweat and tears on the ground behind her along with some dead dragons. She's learned some things that will help you get through whatever you're in the middle of. All I can tell you is it's helping me."
**- Ian Percy**
Founder and President, Emendara LLC, Scottsdale, Arizona


"Lisa has created a way to take the governors off our own engines so that we can realize the full horsepower that we each have inside. It's not the world that holds us back, as this book helps us see impediments that were in our blind spots all along. Slay your dragons and take your success and happiness to new heights."
**- Brian Carruthers**
Author of Building an Empire and Network Marketing Mentor

"By far, the biggest challenge most people have is the battle that is waged in one's own head. With Lisa's new book, you'll learn exactly how to slay that "inner dragon" we all face, put him on his back, and live the rich life you deserve!"

**- Todd Falcone**
Speaker, Trainer and Creator of *Cracking the Code to Success*

"Yet again, Lisa dives deep into the quest of helping you become the best you can be. Her book will help you rise to the glory of your magnificence and live in the kingdom of your own choosing."

**- Tia Crystal**
Visionary Artist

"Lisa's new book is a powerful read that will help you reach your true potential!"

**- Sarah Robbins**
Author of, *Rock Your Network Marketing Business!*

"You no longer have to fear the dragons! Lisa gives you such specific information on just how to conquer them and live your best life. Do not miss this book."

**- Chris Widener**
Author of *The Art of Influence*

"I praise Lisa Jimenez for her authenticity and courage to share her own very real and honest account of personal trials and tribulations. *Slay The Dragon* is a masterful work of truth and beautifully laid blueprint for anyone who has the deep desire to do the work, the courage to pick up the sword and the intent to slay their own dragons. Give your spirit a healing gift and read this book!"

**- Tina Beer**
Ambassador Diamond with It Works Global

"I love Lisa's courage in sharing her own dragons! Her personal examples, blended with her expertise makes this book so powerful. Lisa is a genuine and enthusiastic champion with a servant heart. Her mojo is contagious! I'm honored to call her my "sister".
- **Kelli Rogers**
18 year Network Marketing Leader, Believer & 7 figure income earner enjoying a new adventure with Jeunesse Global

"Lisa walks the talk and has the skeletal remains of her own dragons to prove it. Take heart, take control and take out your saber. Your Dragons are about to disappear! In, *Slay the Dragon* you will learn how to finally take control of your life, learn to live; not just exist, and feel joy in a way that may have eluded you in the past."
- **Heidi Richards Mooney**
CEO - Redhead Marketing, Inc., Publisher - WE Magazine for Women

"*Slay The Dragon* is exactly what Lisa does with this book. We all have Dragons we would like to slay and Lisa has written a simple, thought provoking text to assist us in removing the Dragons that are holding us back. Get this book in the hands of people you care about."
- **Jerry Scribner**
Presidential Director at Stream

"With so many personal development books on the market it's challenging to find one that delivers the goods. Lisa's new book absolutely delivers! If you follow the steps outlined, you will slay your self-limiting dragons and go on to achieve the breakthrough success you deserve."
- **Pamela Barnum**
Former undercover police officer, Federal Crown Prosecutor and author of, *The Law of Confidence*

"Lisa's new book takes us on a journey of self-discovery and teaches us how to become the Dragon Slayer our team and family needs us to be. This is a must-read if you want to become a better leader. I love this book!"
- **Janine Finney**
Co-Author of, *Flip Flop CEO*


"I strongly encourage you to read, *Slay The Dragon* by the best business coach I have ever had! Lisa has helped me break through self-limiting beliefs in the past. Her heart-to-heart transparency inspires and empowers me to press on toward my goals! This will be the book I give my organization to help them reach their potential, too."
- **Michele Lersch**
Double Diamond with It Work Global


"*Slay The Dragon* is a VERY important and valuable book. It can help you become the stronger, more inspiring and successful person you truly want to be. This book delivers clear, confident guidance on exactly how to slay your self-sabotaging "dragons," and every emerging hero needs to read it."
- **Art Burleigh**
Author, trainer, successful affiliate/network marketer and happily married dad and grandfather


"Lisa's deeply personal experience speaks to you in a way that will move you forever. She exemplifies authentic change and her beautiful transparency will inspire you."
- **Lory Muirhead**
Co-author of The Flip Flop CEO

"Lisa Jimenez has a true warrior spirit! Strap on your armor...
pull out your shield...draw your sword...and let the wisdom Lisa
shares in this book help you to bravely go out and slay all of
YOUR dragons!"
- **Sue Cassidy**
Executive National Vice President with Arbonne International


"I had the privilege of working directly with Lisa after reading her remarkable book, *Conquer Fear*.  In the year we spent
coaching together, she taught me the importance of focus and
changing negative belief systems which enabled me to formal-
ize and grow my non-profit ministry and triple my accounting
firm's revenue in two years! Lisa writes and speaks with such
clarity it's as if she reaches deep into your soul and hits the
parts that need to be healed.  In this new book, *Slay the Dragon*,
she delves even deeper into the self-sabotaging behaviors we all
have and guides us through to victory!"
- **Tina Marino**
Founder & Executive Director, The Encouragement Center, Inc.


"Lisa was my first female mentor! Her first book, *Conquer Fear*
helped my team and I have profound breakthroughs. I love her
new book, *Slay the Dragon* as it talks about self-sabotage in a
way that is so authentic and powerful. It will be your guide to
break through any barrier you have."
- **Sarah Zolecki**
Elite 3 Social Marketer with Modere


"As leaders, the number one issue we have to help our people
break through is self-sabotage. Lisa has made our job so much
simpler. Now we can just make sure everyone that enrolls gets a
copy of, *Slay the Dragon*!"
- **Tony Zolecki**
Elite 3 Social Marketer with Modere

"Lisa's authentic, passionate, tenacious, "tell-it-like-it-is" style will keep the pages turning while you read her book, *Slay the Dragon*. This book delivers exceptional insights in a practical way that can generate immediate productivity improvements and a significant boost in your mojo."

**- Rich Razgaitis**
CEO, FloWater

"Lisa is one of a handful of mentors I have; and the only female. Her personal experiences; and not just some theory she came up with; is what makes her so priceless as a coach and mentor. Through, *Slay the Dragon* she is once again giving to other priceless wisdom to provide them a path to conquer their own fears and slay their self-sabotaging dragons."

**- Troy Dooly**
The Beachside CEO, top rated show host and news director at Home Business Radio Network, and Chief Purpose Officer at Lighthouse Idea Crafters

"The Princess has come through with another breakthrough book! Self-sabotage has destroyed more lives and more dreams than any outside force on the planet. Lisa Jimenez's outstanding new work will help millions slay their dragons of self-sabotage. I love the way she ends each chapter with some practical steps that empower us to banish our dragons forever."

**- Vic Johnson**
Founder, AsAManThinketh.net
7-Time Amazon Best Selling Author

"If you want to slay your dragons, read this book. Lisa gives you the armor and sword to make it happen!"

**- Brenda and Scott Schuler**
Young Living Royal Crown Diamonds

"It doesn't take more than one conversation with Lisa Jimenez to recognize how passionate she is about helping others become the very best version of themselves. It's true... the only person who stands in the way of your greatest success is YOU. *Slay the Dragon* will give you all the tools you need to overcome the self-sabotage that is holding you back and encourage you to step into the person you are created to be!"
- **Jordan Maylea Ramirez**
Author of Lifetime of Achievement
Free to Relax Team Leader at Scent-Sations Inc.


"Lisa Jimenez is a true Dragon Slayer. She can teach you how to become one, too. If you're ready to slay them and get out of your own way, read this book!"
- **Donna Krech**
Founder/CEO Thin&Healthy, Inc and WOW Women Conferences


"Anticipate private victories as you integrate the wisdom from Lisa's book. Get ready to slay your Dragons as you unlock your potential and make possible a future not yet imagined."
- **John Crudele**
Professional Speaker


"What Lisa teaches in this book is solid, smart, and doable. I feel fortunate she chose me as her editor, as I learned so much I can apply to my own life."
- **Vicki McCown**
Writer's Coach

"Lisa's book should be required reading for anyone committed to increasing the quality of their life. If you're ready to break through to the next level, read this book."
- **Cynthia Kersey**
Author, Unstoppable & Unstoppable Women and founder & CEO, Unstoppable Foundation


"In the movie, *The Bruce Lee Story* there's a line that says, "If you don't slay your dragons then they will move on to your children." Lisa Jimenez has faced and slain her dragons, some pretty big scary ones, and she shows you how to do it too. Stop the fear, remove the threats, live an abundant life, get… this…book!"
-**Jim Cathcart**
Author of The Acorn Principle


"Lisa's book contains a proven formula for unchaining yourself from everything – everything – that's holding you back. With her intimate understanding of the anatomy of fear, the bold and courageous Lisa Jimenez shows you the exact process for ending self-sabotage!"
-**Margie Aliprandi**
Modere Elite 3 and author of bestseller, *How to Get Absolutely Anything You Want*


"Get your hands on this profound book. Lisa will give you the tools for exactly what you need to slay those dragons and start living a full, happy and exciting life! I know, because she helped me. I attended her Maui Rich Life Mastermind Retreat and launched my "best life" from that experience."
- **Tonya Grimes**
Author and Owner of Solid Success Training

"Lisa has been my business coach for over 3 years. Our weekly calls and daily accountability has been the single most profound boost to my success. I know, from this experience, her new book will be the rocket fuel for your transformation, too."
- **Colleen Riddle**
Platinum with Life Shotz and creator of the *New Mommy Makeover*


"Lisa shares here authentic story of breaking the chains of self-imposed limitations and beliefs. In order to reach your true potential, you must first conquer these limiting beliefs that don't serve you or the world. Lisa's book will help you break through to a better version of you, with inspirational scripture throughout complimenting her insights."
- **Adam Green**
Royal Crown Diamond, Young Living Essential Oils and author of, *25 to Life: Jailbreak Your 9-5 & Escape to Financial Freedom*

# DEDICATION

This book is dedicated with heartfelt love and admiration to:
My three children Auriana, Beau, and Connor.

You three are my favorite people in the world. When I think of what true love is, I think of you. You guys are my healers through tough times and my advocates through great times. No matter what, I always feel loved by you.

As I watch you launch your own independent lives, I smile with much gratitude that you know how to live authentically, boldly, and richly. You are creating wonderful experiences for yourself, and your contribution to others is impressive.
Continue to trust and remain open to God's best plan for you, and you will always be joyful. Expect the best in life and the best will always find you!

Auriana, my favorite memories of you are all the travels we share. Your sense of adventure is such a gift. Wherever you show up in the world, there is magic and pixie dust. I love you.

Beau, my favorite memories of you are all the laughter we share. Your sense of humor and creativity is such a gift. Wherever you are, there is fun and side-splitting laughter. I love you.

Connor, my favorite memories of you are all the friends you welcome into our home. Your sense of community and friendship is such a gift. Wherever you are, there is connection and kinship. I love you.

# ACKNOWLEDGMENTS

Writing a book is definitely a team effort. My team consists of my clients, my Mastermind group, my mentors, and my friends and family.

My clients who allow me to share my wisdom and expertise with the intention of helping them create better lives for themselves. The truth is, the teacher learns the most. As I coach each of you I am transformed. Thank you for your willingness to grow and your commitment to expand what's possible for your life and for your contribution to others. While I've had hundreds of clients contribute to my growth, a special thank you goes to the ones whom I was coaching during the writing of this book:
Carla Burns, James Montgomerie, Mary-Lee Widder, Yvonne Ortega, Susan Kimball, Anita and Vince Lamberti, Stephanie Clark, Fredrik Ankarsköld, Cameron and Roben Green, Joseph Ranseth, Tricia Garton; and to my Life Shotz leaders that I coach every week: Colleen Riddle, Kevin Garver, Isabel Acosta, Tracy Teel, Larry Thill, Sarah Young, Kari Atkinson, TJ Bates, and Polly Altizer.

My Mastermind group who continue to expand what's possible for me. Your willingness to share your wisdom and be tough on me makes me better. Thank you to Randy Gage, Bob Burg, Kathy Zader, Gina Carr, Terry Brock, JB Glossinger, Bruce Turkel, and our favorite spirit, Joachim DePosada, who lives on in our hearts.

My mentors who coach me and offer their wisdom and expertise. Your generosity of time and effort that you pour into me is both humbling and exhilarating. Thank you for who you are: Randy Gage, Richard Brooke, Gary Peters, and Bob Proctor.

My mentors from Bliss Retreat (The Fierce Fourteen) were the group of people who helped cause the breakthrough I needed to write this book. Sitting in that hot seat (the love nest) and breaking through my fears and insecurities was possible only because of your ability to hold the space of love, power, and possibility. You are amazing people. Thank you for your candor and love: Richard Brooke, Kimmy Brooke, Brenda Schuler, Kimber King, Janine Finney, Lory Muirhead, Jennifer Ampuja, Geralyn Kamaha'olani Camarillo, Arna Johnson, Robyn Murrah, Megan Baldwin, Kelli Rogers, and Margie Aliprandi.

My editor and writing coach who makes me so much better. Vicki McCown, you are a gem. Your expertise gives me the freedom to write without barriers, knowing you will work your magic and clean it up for me.

My friends who just "get me." Thank you for your unconditional love: Robyn Nassetta, Cecilia and Gary Peters, Geri Emmetts, Jana Carabino, Renee Harper, Lori Flesher, Tracy Teel, and Peter Schlosser.

My family who is the foundation of who I am: Phil and Helen Kelly, Renee Kelly LaVelle, Chuck Kelly, and Scott Kelly.

My amazing boyfriend who is my adventurous partner and my soft place to land. Dave Skelton, you've introduced me to SCUBA diving, sailing the BVIs, piloting a 737 airplane (in a simulator), rock climbing, and experiencing levels of my adventurous spirit that I didn't even know I had. It is a pleasure and a privilege to love you.

# FOREWARD

Lisa and I met while collaborating on *Crafting Your Vision* with the illustrious Randy Gage. What struck me initially about Lisa were her poise, passion, and purpose. She had a clear vision of who she intended to become; an inspiring vision of a woman on fire destined to lift millions of others into their own power.

Lisa, like all humans, carried around some chatter about how scary her path might be. What trumped the chatter was her core drive to "Do It Anyway." And this is the very distinction that separates the "dos" from the "do nots"…doing it anyway.

Lisa has embraced her fears and self-sabotaging chatter for all things, from dating, falling in love, speaking to audiences of thousands, and publishing blogs and books to building a successful network marketing residual income. Through it all, Lisa has crafted new visions that she decided were more important to her than her "BS." She chose those new visions every day and in every way. She rose to them and she manifested the beautiful results.

This is not a book about theory written by someone that just wanted to have a book. This is Lisa's life work in process. I have had the honor of watching Lisa Jimenez slay her dragons over and over for the past 15 years. Her life is the laboratory. Her willingness to share with an authentic and fearless heart is a gift to others. Her message is priceless work. When you take on her process—you and Lisa—can change your life…into anything *your* heart desires.
- **Richard Bliss Brooke**
Author, *Mach II, The Art of Vision and Self Motivation* and *The Four Year Career*

# INTRODUCTION

## *Where Did My MoJo Go?*

"Enough! I am so over this!" I yelled out in to the silence of the morning. It had been nearly seven years since I went through the financial pain of losing my homes to foreclosure and short sales. It had been almost a decade since the dissolution of my 18-year marriage. And yet, I was still living the pain of those experiences every day. I had taken on an identity of failure, and it was affecting everything I did—or didn't do. In other words, self-sabotage was running my life!

This is what self-sabotage looked like for me:

After the foreclosures, I continued to run my businesses, except I was so risk-adverse, the projects I took on were way below my usual standard. After the divorce, I continued to enjoy my personal life, but I was riddled with fear of loss.

I questioned—deeply questioned—my desire for the material and even considered becoming a minimalist (that's actually funny, given how much I love to live well), and I renounced the material and the desires of my heart. I decided those things brought too much pain and it was better to not want them. (Unless you are truly called to be a minimalist, this is where all of you underachievers cheer for my enlightenment and together we celebrate how spiritual we are!)

Obviously, I now believe that decision was just one of the ways I was sabotaging and keeping myself small. For me, small meant safe; and after being beat up in life, feeling safe was all I wanted. However, with every passing day, I became more and more agitated. The so-called safety I was seeking began to feel like a prison in which I'd been given a life sentence. And the craziest thing of all—I was the one who had pronounced that sentence on myself. I remember sharing with a group of friends at the Bliss Retreat, "I feel like I've lost my MoJo."

That last statement couldn't have been more true! I had lost my MoJo. Self-sabotage was keeping me from my calling of leading people to discover their greatness, because I was keeping myself from discovering my own!

The book you hold in your hand tells the story of HOW I became a Dragon Slayer, got my MoJo back, and how you can, too.

May this message richly bless and inspire you,

*Lisa*

Lisa Jimenez M.Ed.
Delray Beach, Florida ~ 2015

# Contents

# Chapter 1:

## *The Birth of a Dragon*

Alicia knew what she wanted. She set a goal and started to move toward that goal, and yet...something was keeping her from advancing.

Paul was an experienced entrepreneur. He was involved in several startups. And yet...something always took him out of the game.

Carl's dream of building a multimillion dollar company became a reality... and yet, he didn't feel successful or fulfilled.

Have you set a goal, and yet...something is getting in your way? Do you know what you want, and yet...something or someone seems to be holding you back? You can see this happening, but you haven't quite pinpointed the culprit.

Let's get right to it. The culprit that holds you back is You.

You allow fear and self-doubt to get in the way. You let other people and their opinions hold you back. You secretly blame others, society, or the economy for your mediocrity. The reality is you have been sabotaging your own success.

The definition of sabotage is: to deliberately undermine, damage, or attack a plan or activity.

Why would you ever deliberately undermine, damage, or attack your own dreams?

The answer is you can't help yourself! You sabotage your own dreams because your subconscious mind is programmed at failure. Your mindset screams mediocrity. You are wired to struggle.

Self-sabotage is a tool of the subconscious. It lives in the hidden parts of your mind and most of the time you are not even aware you are sabotaging yourself.

So, while your conscious mind knows what you want to achieve, your subconscious mind is not in agreement. This lack of alignment gives birth to the Dragons of Self-Sabotage. And no amount of skill training, goal setting, or will power can break the habitual pattern of sabotage.

### The 5 Dragons of Self-Sabotage

*DRAGON #1:* **The Dragon of Limiting Self-View**

*DRAGON #2:* **The Dragon of Circumstances**

*DRAGON #3:* **The Dragon of Fear**

*DRAGON #4:* **The Dragon of Ambiguity**

*DRAGON #5:* **The Dragon of Efforting**

These Dragons of Self-Sabotage show up in subtle ways, but they definitely leave clues. Here are some examples of what the Dragons look like in your life:

If you want to double or triple your income, yet you have a mindset that money will create pain, is evil, or you're not good at managing it, you have a Dragon.

If you want to become a leader, but you have the fear of disappointing others or a fear of being judged, you have a Dragon.

If you want to launch your own business, but you have an "employee mentality," you have a Dragon.

If you want to be in an exclusive relationship or get married, but you hold the belief men/women cannot be trusted or you are not lovable or capable of monogamy, you have a Dragon.

If you want to lose weight, but you hold the belief that it's not safe to be fit or it's not spiritual to give attention to yourself, you have a Dragon.

If you want to enjoy the journey, but your subconscious is programmed that life is hard or that struggling is noble, you have a Dragon.


Do you notice the pattern demonstrated in all of these Dragons? What is the one common feature they share? All of these Dragons represent "a gap."

The Dragons of Self-Sabotage are the gap between who you are today and who you want to become. The good news is this gap is normal and is your opportunity to grow into a better version of you!

So, when you set a goal that is outside your comfort zone (let's sure hope it is!), your subconscious mind detects a disharmony and alarms go off as if an impending danger has just been presented. The subconscious mind springs into action to do whatever it takes to pull you back to your current mindset and the "safety" of your programming. It doesn't matter if your goal is good for you or not; to the subconscious mind, every goal represents disharmony and must be stopped. The most effective tactic the subconscious uses to stop you (also known as keeping you the same) is with The Dragons of Self-Sabotage.

Every goal worth achieving creates a disharmony—at first. The problem arises when you stay in the disharmony or let it pull you back to your comfort zone. You've got to be willing to accept this uncomfortable stage and do the inner work to create harmony between your conscious and subconscious mind.

I know for certain you can achieve any goal, any dream you have for yourself. I've seen it happen in hundreds of my coaching clients and I've experienced it myself. The one commonality with all our success stories is we were willing to do the "inner work" to reprogram the subconscious mind. **We became the person who lives our dream life from the inside out.**

We now have a formula for how you slay the Dragons of Self-Sabotage. That formula is the process of reprogramming the subconscious mind to align with your goals and dreams and fill in the gap between where you are now and where you want to be.

**The Dragon Slayer Formula:** Hold the vision of what you want and do the inner work to reprogram your subconscious mind to align with that vision.

The Dragon Slayer formula is the good news within this book. The bad news is that formula can get messy; really messy... And that's where we will pick it up in Chapter 2.

# Chapter 2:

## *Dragon #1:*
## *How to Slay the Dragon of Limiting Self-View*

It seemed to be a great childhood nickname to everyone in my family. The very definition means royalty and of noble descent. However, the nickname Duchess wasn't royal to me at all. I had an older sister whose nickname was Princess. So the title of Duchess in my three-year-old mind surely meant "second place."

Your perception of a nickname or any type of label from your childhood holds great power. The meaning you give those labels, titles, and nicknames creates a self-view that can either empower you or destroy you.
The nickname Duchess and the perception of second place had a profound impact on my behaviors as a kid. In youth I was quite involved in 4H and participated in several state fair competitions. In all of these contests I always got the red ribbon. You probably know, the red ribbon is second place.

In middle school I picked up gymnastics and entered various county Olympics. In every competition, I was most awarded the silver medal. As you know, the silver medal is second place.
Then, in my latter teens and early twenties I joined the pageant world. During intermission of the Miss Teen USA pageant, the reigning queen came to me and said, "You've got this, Lisa. You just have to give a great speech and you're going to win." The speech portion of the competition was my strength. But when I took the stage, the words to my speech didn't come with me. I knew I didn't deserve to win. So when it came time

to announce the winner, my name was called as "first runner up." That sounded pretty good. I was getting closer to the word "first." But as we all know, first runner up is another way of saying "second place"!

My subconscious mind was set at second place and my results matched that programming. This program told me, "Be successful, but not too successful." "Be good, but not too good." Second place was my comfort zone and matched my self-view. Please notice how, even with getting a red ribbon, silver medal, and first runner up, I still placed. You can accomplish a lot with a limiting self-view. But also notice how that limiting self-view kept me from fully experiencing my potential.

You'll live a pretty good life with okay results and average happiness with your current self-view; but you wouldn't be reading this book if that was acceptable to you. No, you're different. You want SO MUCH MORE than average or mediocrity.

## How the Subconscious Mind Creates a Mindset

When you were conceived, you were pure potential. At the moment of conception you are nothing and everything. Just sit with that for a minute. Just consider what pure potential really means. Albert Einstein coined the term "zero-point energy" in his research in physics to define the pure potential of nothing. When you have nothing, what else do you have?

When you have nothing, you have everything.

In regards to creating a personality or a mindset, zero-point energy is a ground state of what is possible. In other words, ANYTHING IS POSSIBLE!

The exciting part I want you to understand is in zero-point energy something WILL get created and will continue to evolve. (For more information about zero-point energy, study Niels Bohr, physicist and 1922 Nobel Prize recipient.)

So back to you... Here you are at conception and then birth, in zero-point energy (this space of full potential), and something happened...

Life happened. Circumstances occurred. Experiences arose.

In your early years, you experienced all kinds of events. Before your seventh birthday, your brain has not developed the ability for rational thought. So, your young mind makes things up. You give meaning to everything that happens to you. You don't have the gift of reason to discern the significance of what happened. With your pre-rational brain, what you make up is limiting, scary, and exaggerated. Your subconscious mind takes the meaning and develops a mindset, similar to software that runs a computer. Then, this mindset (software) causes you to behave in certain ways. These behaviors create patterns. You continue to repeat these patterns over and over and over again. (Remember zero-point energy: Something gets created and it continues to evolve itself.) You attract more circumstances that affirm this negative mindset.

I'm not good enough. Life is hard. I'm too small to matter. I can be happy, but not too happy. Drama or illness gives me attention. If I win, someone else loses. There's not enough. Don't show off. Poverty is spiritual. All of these core beliefs create your subconscious programming. And this programming was created by the seven-year-old version of you!

### *You Can Never "Out-Succeed" Your Self-View*

One of the first steps to slay the Dragon of Limiting Self-View is to identify all the labels, nicknames, and decisions you've made about yourself. Answer the following questions and notice the patterns.

What was your childhood nickname or label? What was the decision you made about yourself with the labels and nicknames you were given?

_____
_____
_____

Another helpful exercise to identify your self-view is to look at your life today, right now, and ask yourself the following: (Step out of yourself and answer the following questions from that perspective.)

Describe the self-view a person with my level of happiness would have.

_____
_____
_____

Describe the self-view a person with my bank account would have.

_____
_____
_____

Describe the self-view a person with my level of success, joy, and fulfillment would have.

_____
_____
_____

How to Slay Dragon #1: The Dragon of Limiting Self-View
Your childhood nickname, the perception you had about where you fit in, and the meaning you gave to things that happened all created your self-view. You just got present to what your self-view currently is with the exercises above.
Now, answer this question: SO WHAT?

I had you write down all of the answers above so you could complete the next step of this very important exercise. Take a different colored pen and write over your answers the following statement in big, bold letters:

IT'S A NEW DAY

Your self-view was created for you, not by you! Things happened in your childhood and your subconscious mind made them mean something. Lacking rational thought, your young mind could not discern the difference between your perception of what happened and the truth of what happened. You simply did not have the capability to logically choose what to believe in the forming of your personality and your original self-view.

It's a new day. Today, as an adult, you have the gift of rational thought. The intellectual faculty of reason gives you the power to choose what you believe about yourself no matter what others say or what your current results reveal.

Who do you say you are now?

Science teaches the incredible odds of your unique design in conception. Theology teaches you are created in the image of God. Psychology teaches the unlimited potential of your mind. I loved hearing Jim Carrey's 2014 commencement speech at Maharishi University in which he referenced the famous quote of the French philosopher and Jesuit priest, Pierre Teilhard de Chardin:

"You are not a soul living in a limited body. You are a body living in a limitless, boundless soul."

When you see yourself as a spiritual being who is having a human experience, everything changes. You have free will to choose this belief. Choosing a spiritual perspective means you see yourself as a limitless, powerful, and expansive.

It matters less what you used to believe about yourself and more about what you believe now. Stop letting your seven-year-old self-view run your life. It's a new day. It's time for a new you.

The sword to slay the Dragon of Limiting Self-View is a hope of an expansive future and the will to declare who you say you are now...and then now...and in every moment.

## *The Power of a Declaration*

You must declare who you say you are. A declaration is an empowering thought combined with emotion that you speak out loud. Declarations are powerful tools that retrain your brain and reprogram your subconscious mind.

We have an example of the power of a declaration in marriage. Two people stand before a pastor, priest, rabbi, or justice of the peace who proclaims, "With the power invested in me, I declare you husband and wife."

Our Founding Fathers ushered in our freedom from Britain with the Declaration of Independence.

We understand the power of a declaration in theology. In the book of Genesis it reads that God declared, "Let there be light." And there was light.

You have this same power within you with the spoken word. Your word creates your world. Tap into the power of a declaration and just watch who you become.

Here are a few of my favorite declarations that have helped me reprogram my subconscious mind and change my self-view:

**I Am Divinely Guided.** It's like I have a supernatural GPS constantly moving me in the right direction. I am always in the right place at the right time. It's so much fun when I relax in this guidance. I love it when I realize the serendipity of all the events in my life! Things just always come together for me...

**Everything Is Always Working Out for Me.**  It is amazing how in sync I am with my highest good. Even when an opportunity, a partner, or an idea goes away, I immediately get a better one. I love how evident it is that my life is getting better and better. I notice how quickly a no is replaced with a yes. I am grateful when a new and better idea comes to me. All things are working out for me...

**Every Day in Every Way, I'm Getting Better and Better.**  I love the progress in my life and in myself. I notice how good I'm getting at my people skills, my presentation skills, my leadership skills. It's so gratifying to see the evidence of my progress. I wake up every day knowing I'm getting better and better, closer and closer to the person I want to be—the person who lives my best life. I love focusing on my progress and feel great satisfaction in who I am becoming. I am having fun focusing on my progress. It's exciting to know every day in every way I'm getting better and better.

I trust you are beginning to understand the power you have in changing your self-view and ultimately your life. Train yourself to be aware of your thoughts and speak your empowering declarations.

You BECOME what you think about. You ATTRACT what you BECOME.

## *Fredrick's Story*

The Costa Rica Mastermind Retreat was only two weeks away. People from several countries were gathering together for six days of mastermind to cause a breakthrough in their lives. Fredrick, one of the participants, was not aware his breakthrough would come before the retreat even began.

"I can't come to the retreat," Fredrick, said as soon as I answered the phone.

"What happened?" I asked. He began to tell me about an event in his past which was keeping him from getting the required visa to come to Costa Rica.

"Even though I already bought my airline ticket," he continued, "the airlines won't honor it without the visa."

I've travelled internationally enough to know he was right. I asked him a few questions about exactly what happened in his past that kept the government from granting the visa. When he was done telling me the story I said, "That is not who you are anymore, Fredrick! I've been coaching you for over a year, and I know who you are. It's time to transform your past and slay the Dragon of Self-View."

Then I asked him a defining question, "Who do you say that you are?"

Fredrick, had been working with me long enough to know his declarations, and he began speaking them with conviction.

"I am a man of my word. I am loving, kind, and compassionate. I am a powerful contributor who makes a difference in the world," he declared.

Fredrick, was being given an opportunity to prove his new declarations. As we hung up, I gave him his assignment. "Take a stand for who you have re-created yourself to be. Go back to the agency or the airlines or whomever you need to talk to as that man and get yourself to Costa Rica."

One of the most amazing moments of that retreat was getting his phone call at 3:30 in the morning from the lobby of the Four Seasons Costa Rica Hotel saying, "I'm here, Lisa. I made it!"

What about you? Are you ready to slay the Dragon of your limiting self-view? Let go of the labels, nicknames, and memories that limit you. It's a new day and you have the power with your declarations to change everything.

Stop declaring that you are shy, broken, challenged, or handicapped. Quit declaring that you don't have what it takes or you have no time or money. These declarations are not serving you. They leave no room for something new to be created. Limiting declarations just create more of the same.

Who do you say you are? Train your subconscious mind to align with your new self-view with your empowering declarations. Declare your empowering beliefs:

_____

_____

_____

Remember, in the process of slaying the Dragon of Limiting Self-View you need both the hope of a new possibility and your will to declare it.

My son Connor reminded me of this in his explanation of the comic book about The Green Lantern. That super hero, who fights with the green ring of will power, became unstoppable only when partnered with the Blue Lantern, whose super power is the blue ring of hope. Will and Hope made the powers of these super heroes invincible.

And so it is in your life... Will power partnered with hope makes you powerful beyond measure.

For me, my hope is my relationship with God. The single most effective ritual I have is spending time in prayer and meditation every morning. This is where my declarations are created and my self-view expands.

God is the kindest person I know. I am overwhelmed by His generosity. I ask for the Holy Spirit's anointing over my day every morning and watch and enjoy that anointing in supernatural ways throughout the day.

Putting your hope in God is your personal choice. For me, I choose this belief. I cultivate my relationship with God daily; and attribute my freedom, authenticity, confidence and all of my success to that decision.

One of my favorite quotes by an anonymous philosopher is: "You are free to struggle but you don't have to struggle to be free."

You are free... You are so free you can even choose struggle, bondage, and a limiting life. You have the gift of free will. You get to choose what you believe about God, your life, and about who you are. Through the power of your mind and the gift of free will, you get to choose to believe the best about who you are and what is possible for you. Through the power of your heart you can choose to believe you are highly favored, anointed, and more than enough.

Choose well and know there are always second chances, and third, and fourth...

Think about a kid who really messed up in his youth or someone who had a history of bad breaks. Then, things began to turn around for him. Something started to happen. He began experiencing some success. That success created more of the same. After a while, everything he touched seemed to turn to gold, as though he had a magical light shining on him or he were favored in some way. Luck followed him everywhere.

How did that person turn his unlucky life around?

What happened had nothing to do with luck. That person chose to transform his self-view, one declaration at a time.

When I reprogrammed my subconscious mind to "first place," my behaviors changed and results followed. And guess what? The real breakthrough came when I wasn't concerned with either place. It wasn't about first place or second place anymore. It was about showing up excited to live life at my full potential and experience the favor and good fortune I expected in life.

You become what you declare yourself to be. You attract what you become. You get what you expect.

## Dream Home

When I was married and building our first home, my husband and I went way over budget. As the move-in date drew near, I did my best not to lose my excitement by the fact that we had no money for furniture.

"It's okay that we don't have a dining room table," I told myself. "We'd probably never use it anyway." "We don't need a family room sofa," I said to the kids. "We'll get to watch movies on the floor."

All I kept thinking about was how grateful I was for this home and how the 18-month building process was finally over and we were moving in. Then, two days before our move-in date, the phone rang. A friend of ours, a general contractor, had some interesting news for us. He had just closed on his fully furnished spec home and had the new owners eager to move in the very next day. The problem was they had all their own furniture and wanted the house vacant for their move-in. The next thing I knew our contractor friend said, "If you can get a moving van here in the next few hours, you can have all of the furniture!"

We were given a house full of beautiful, brand new furniture as a gift for our new home. Just like that we went from sitting on the floor to setting up house—a fully furnished house.

### Lost in Paris

I rented a flat in Paris for the summer. One day I decided to go exploring without a map or an itinerary. I jumped on the Metro and began my adventure. I had a great time discovering new museums and hidden art galleries, new piazzas, unique stores, and out-of the-way restaurants. Hours went by. As dinnertime neared, I decided I'd better get back to my flat. When I began to retrace my steps, the route looked so different. Paris, like many European cities, changes its dynamics from daytime to evening and nothing looked familiar. I began to feel anxious as the evening moved into night and I couldn't find my way back to my flat.

And then I stopped myself from going down that negative path and quieted my mind. Within a few minutes I felt an inner knowing of the correct path to take. Without hesitation, I jumped on the Metro and trusted I was on the right train. Not only had I picked the correct Metro line, a three-piece band shared the same car and began playing my favorite Frank Sinatra song, "Fly Me to the Moon." I relaxed into the melody and began singing with my new friends. Before the song ended, familiar sights came into view. I smiled, knowing I was almost home. That experience was another confirmation that I am always taken care of.

When you truly believe you are the type of person that great things happen to, you allow yourself to take more risks. Your willingness to take risks and stay positive (even if it looks like what you decided is not working) is a character trait that you can choose to have. Develop your risk-taking ability begins with an developing an empowering self-view.

## Dan's Story

My friend developed innovative software technology in the mid 1980s. He received a call from a predominant company in the industry asking him to visit their headquarters to discuss developing specific touch-screen technology for them.

He thanked them for the opportunity and then answered with five words he regrets to this day: "That's not my area of expertise." The opportunity passed him by. Logically, it wasn't his area of expertise. But in the realm of possibility, serendipity, and risk-taking, just imagine what could have happened if he would have said yes to sitting down with that company and discovering who he could become to match his skill with what they were looking for.

Your New, Empowering Self-View Helps Others

I was asked to be one of the speakers on the Bob Proctor Cruise. Bob Proctor, an icon in the personal development industry, is one of my mentors and friends. As grateful as I was, the first thought that came to my mind was "I'm not ready to speak among the other professional speakers and thought leaders." However, instead of allowing the Dragon of Limiting Self-View to control my behaviors, I retrained those thoughts and disciplined my mind with the reality that I would not have been asked if Bob and his team didn't think I was ready. I hired a speaking coach and elicited help writing and practicing my message.

Weeks before we were to set sail, I received an email from Bob Proctor's office. There were 30 cabins still available. Bob had decided to give them to each speaker's guests instead of creating one last push to sell out. His generosity wowed me. I quickly sent out invitations to my coaching clients and invited them to the Bob Proctor Cruise; with all expenses paid. I shared that they could stay at my home the night before and I would rent a limo to take us to the ship. Within a few hours, 13 of my clients from all over the world—France, New Zealand, Canada, Sweden, The Netherlands, and America—responded with a resounding "Yes!"

I never felt such power and joy as I did being able to share that cruise with my coaching clients. We were forever changed from the experience. It could only have happened when I was willing to slay the Dragon of Self-View, accept an opportunity that I thought was too big for me, and allow myself to be a vessel of good fortune.

Your willingness to slay the Dragon of self-view matters! Who you become along the way makes a difference for not only you, but for the people in your life. Slay the Dragon of Limiting Self-View and you will become a person who greatly influences and benefits others.

## *Dragon #1: The Dragon of Limiting Self-View*

**THE SWORD:** Will

**THE PROCESS:** With your WILL you choose what you think, believe, and declare about yourself. Through rituals and daily disciplines, you declare who you are. You become who you declare yourself to be.

**THE RESULT:** Your subconscious is now aligned with your declarations. You attract the ideas, people, and opportunities that mirror your new and empowering self-view.

**The Dragon Slayer Formula:** Hold the vision of what you want and do the inner work to reprogram your subconscious mind to align with that vision.

In the next chapter, we'll slay Dragon #2: The Dragon of Circumstances. Until then, declare who you are, practice your new habits, expect the best, and enjoy the process of re-creating your self-view and your life.

# Chapter 3:

## *How to Slay Dragon #2:*
## *The Dragon of Circumstances*

I walked into my home to the cheery voices of my three children calling out, "Mom's home!" I smiled as I watched them run toward me with excitement, and we hugged and laughed until we fell over. I had been in Sweden for a speaking engagement and away for nearly a week. Mark, my husband of 18 years, kissed me and said, "Welcome home." I felt something sad with his energy but had no idea how extreme that sadness was until later. After all the gifts were opened and the kids had settled in to watch a movie, he asked me to come into the study.

"Lisa," he began with a quivering voice, "you know I haven't been happy in our marriage for the past year."

I nodded and whispered, "I know." We had been to a counselor several times throughout the year.

"While you were gone I found an apartment, and I'm going to move out."

I sat there speechless, searching for words, the perfect words. No words came. I began crying uncontrollably. Then I said the only thing I could think of to say.

"Don't quit on me, Mark. You've got to fight for me. Fight for us!" I shouted. He looked up at me with so much sadness and whispered, "I don't have the fight in me."

Mark did move out that night. I was devastated. For weeks I fasted, prayed, and asked God to restore my marriage. I went to see a Christian counselor twice a week. If Mark didn't have the fight in him, I would fight enough for the both of us.

At our fourth or fifth session, the counselor looked at me and asked, "Does Mark want to be married to you, Lisa?" What a dumb question, I thought, and reluctantly answered, "No." She opened up the Bible and read something about how God wants peace. It was gibberish to me. Then she asked me a question that rocked me to my core. "If Mark doesn't want to be married to you anymore, why are you holding on so tightly?" I was shocked by her question and thought it was the most ludicrous thing I'd ever heard! I couldn't believe that question was coming from a Christian counselor. I got up and walked out of her office, thinking to myself, "She is the worst counselor in the world!"

As I drove away something began to stir in me. I thought about the counselor's words again, "Live in peace," and the haunting question, "Why are you holding on so tightly?"

The truth broke me at that day. I sat in the car and began sobbing. I was holding on and forcing a reconciliation; and finally realized why.

If I got a divorce, everything I believed in would be a lie. All the truths and doctrines I based my life on would be wrong. And, worst of all, I would be a fraud for believing in it. I knew logically this was not true, but subconsciously I was completely broken. I was riddled with guilt and humiliation from what I believed divorce meant about me—a born again Christian.

I turned my car around and went back to the counselor's office. That was the defining moment that changed everything. With the help from that counselor, I did the work to transform the meaning I was giving divorce and let go of a marriage that was not meant to be anymore.

My belief about what divorce meant made it nearly impossible for me to accept it. Until I changed that belief I would continue to force a reconciliation or suffer greatly from being a failure and a fraud.

I chiseled away at this destructive meaning by replacing it with an empowering truth. Divorce meant I had a second chance. I was free to live more authentically. It meant I was single and could even date again if I chose to. I had been given a new opportunity to recreate myself and design the rest of my life. Over time the new meaning was that divorce is a gift.

I continued to do the inner work to reprogram my subconscious mind and the meaning I gave divorce. Several months went by; and as my new empowering beliefs took root, the suffering began to diminish. The healing had begun.

### The Benefits of Trauma

It is easier to reprogram your subconscious mind with a traumatic experience like divorce, health or financial issues, or a job loss. Why? Because trauma puts you in a zero-point energy. (Review this teaching in Chapter 2). With a traumatic experience, you have no strength to keep a limiting identity, labels, or expectations in place. With trauma, you finally release control and show up with nothing, which is the most powerful state of mind to create. When you have nothing, you have everything.

Hardships, financial struggles, divorce, health issues, and life's hard knocks happen to everyone. The fascinating truth is this: it's not the circumstance that holds you back. It's the meaning you give to that circumstance that causes the destruction. What you choose to make that circumstance mean (good or bad) creates the quality of your life.

Don't stay in a rut of excuses. Stop being a victim. It is not your nationality, age, gender, or genetics that cause negative circumstances. And it's not your circumstances that hold you back. Shift the meaning you give them. Circumstances are your opportunity to grow into the person you could be—a man/woman of strength, wisdom, and grace.

When you do the inner work that your negative circumstances are calling you to do, you receive the gift of transformation that they hold.

## *A Breakdown Leads to a Breakthrough*

One day, while driving my kids home from school, I received a call from Janet, my decorator. The kids and I had moved into a new house after the divorce and Janet was helping me make it a home.

"I found a piece of art in your storage garage that fits perfectly in the living room. It's like this piece of art was made for this house," she said.

I couldn't think of which piece of art she was referring to, but when we walked into the house, I looked at it hanging on my wall and felt my knees buckle. It was a painting I had done to help me heal from the divorce. The painting was an impressionist piece that depicted my marriage and kids in a large circle— so large it covered two canvases that were meant to be hung together. My decorator had separated the two pieces and hung them with a gaping void of empty space in between.

"The circle is broken," I cried. "My family is broken!" I fell to the floor in a mess of pain. My daughter, Auriana, who was 13 years old at the time, put her arm around me and said, "Mommy, the circle isn't broken. It's just bigger! And all this space…" She pointed to the void between the two canvases. "… is where more people will come in and love us."

I looked into my daughter's eyes and chose to believe her. Auriana, as well as my two boys, Beau and Connor, were my healers during that difficult time. Those words from Auriana and the vision she casted before me was the defining moment of my breakthrough.

## What Is a Breakthrough?

The definition of a breakthrough is: a sudden increase in understanding. The verb context of breakthrough is: to open the way for a new development to occur.

In every breakthrough there is a breaking down...

Breakthroughs are messy. Many people are not willing to be with their sadness, frustration, or anger. They do not have the capacity to face their pain and suffering. So they drift through life numbing their feelings and causing their passions to dissolve into mediocrity.

Don't let that be you. Have the courage to face and deal with the messiness of a breakdown; it's your access to a breakthrough!

Causing a breakthrough involves telling the truth about what's not working in your life. Tell the truth about what you really want and the limiting beliefs you have about those desires. Be real about your insecurities. Your authenticity is the first place to start. Then, you will grapple with a concept or belief in your inner thoughts. This inner battle is uncomfortable; but *this is the process* of retraining the brain. Your breakthrough will come from your willingness to stay in the inquiry, keep noticing and replacing limiting beliefs, and accept the process of transformation.

All public victories are preceded by private ones.

With every break down you now have an opening for a breakthrough. You made space for a new possibility in your life.

## *Breaking Out and Breaking Into a Second Chance*

A few days after my breakthrough, I went outside in my backyard to enjoy the cool autumn morning. I opened my journal and wrote the questions, "If I could be, do, and have anything in life, what would it be? What lights me up?"

Instantly pictures came to my mind. With great enthusiasm and newfound confidence, I started to write.

1. Luxury Travel — Experiencing the beauty of this world in exotic cities around the globe in luxury.

2. Stimulating Conversation — Sharing ideas and discussing what's possible in life with like-minded people and creating a deep connection with each other.

3. Making a Difference — Having a profound impact on another person that radically transforms their life and makes them feel loved, inspired, and empowered.

As soon as I had written down those three core values, an image bounced off the page and I shouted, "That's Rich Life Mastermind Retreats!" I knew to my core this was what I truly wanted to do with my life. I felt inspired to make this dream happen and, even though I was scared, I immediately went into action. I got online and booked a ticket to Paris, France, where I knew the first retreat would take place.

I spent three incredible days in Paris the very next weekend and designed the entire Mastermind retreat. I booked the hotel rooms and the meeting rooms; reserved the restaurants and excursions; spoke with owners of cooking schools and art studios and planned innovative and unique excursions for my group. I even met the tenor of the Paris Opera House and arranged to have him serenade us one of the evenings.

The vision was so clear. I saw us walk out of our hotel to a stretch limo waiting for us. As we step inside the limo the tenor begins belting out an aria from a famous opera. We drive along the Champs Elysees and the Rue de Rivoli, past the Eiffel Tower, touring Paris in a limousine while sipping champagne and being serenaded in different languages from the talented tenor.

I saw all of the participants sharing ideas and contributing to each other's breakthroughs. I heard the laughter, saw the smiles, and envisioned the results these breakthroughs would cause.

I flew home from Paris (having put $15,000 on my credit card) ready for my first Mastermind retreat. There was only one thing missing. I had no clients! I didn't even have a website or marketing material.

What I did have was DESIRE...a burning desire to launch my new life through this business adventure. Within six weeks I had a solid business plan, marketing campaign, website, business cards, and brochures.

Three months went by. Everything for the retreat had been put in place, but still no clients had registered. I should have asked myself: Did I take on more than I could handle? However, that question never came to my mind. I had already experienced the worst thing that could ever happen to me: divorce. If I survived that, I could survive anything! I felt unstoppable.

Then, the phone rang…

I picked up the phone and heard a lovely voice on the other end say, "My name is Lilja Prieur from Namibia, Africa. I bought your book, *Conquer Fear!*, and I am calling to find out if you take on international coaching clients."

"Yes, I do," I replied. "Tell me about yourself and what you want to create."

She proceeded to tell me she wanted to write a book about her experience of escaping apartheid in Namibia. Her goal was to inspire people to believe in their dreams. She continued to share more about her life and then said, "After I escaped Namibia, I was given a free education and am now living in…Paris, France!"

I nearly dropped the phone. She was living in the same city where my first Mastermind retreat was being held. Lilja registered for that first retreat and has participated in several since then.

Lilja's call was a confirmation to me. It was God's way of telling me I was on the right track and the new life I was creating—after divorce—was going to be magnificent.

Nine months after that cool autumn morning, where I wrote down my core values, I was in Paris with eight other entrepreneurs hosting my first Rich Life Mastermind Retreat.

## *Cause Your Breakthrough*

What are the challenges, heartaches, and circumstances you have experienced? Most importantly, what did you make them mean?

Get present to this list of all the limiting meanings and realize you can give yourself permission to give each one a new and empowering meaning.

Here are some examples:
The meaning I used to give divorce was "I failed." Now, I make the circumstance mean "I am free."
The meaning I used to give my failure in business was "I'm not good in business." Now, I make the circumstance mean "I am more educated to make and keep more profits!"
The meaning I used to give bankruptcy or financial struggle was "I'm not worthy of money." Now, I make it mean "I now have the opportunity to believe my wealth is being restored!"
The meaning I used to give disease was "I'm weak." Now, I make the circumstance mean "I master balance and well-being!"
Your circumstances are given to you to cause a breakthrough and experience that part of you that's powerful beyond measure.

**WARNING:** The greatest danger in transforming the Dragon of Circumstances is the addiction to overcoming. This can give you such a high that you begin attracting more problems and opportunities to feel the rush that comes from being a survivor. Many people find their identity in their negative circumstance. They become their struggle. They become the illness. They actually identify who they are with their circumstance.

Never collapse your circumstance with who you are.
You are not divorce or rejection.

You are not financial struggle.
You are not illness.
You are not depression.

Andy got the diagnosis of colon cancer and beat it within six months. He created a total immersion healing experience and poured all of his intellect, emotions, and spiritual power into healing his body. When he got the news he was cancer free, something interesting happened. Instead of moving on and getting back to his life, he continued to act like a cancer patient. He had collapsed his circumstance with himself and attracted another diagnosis. It wasn't until he created a distinction between his circumstance and himself that he could truly be free.

Distinguish the difference between you and your challenge. Stop finding your identity or your value in your circumstances.

Let's play a mental game to slay the Dragon of Circumstances without becoming addicted to the kill.

### Mind Game #1:
Picture your circumstance as a red ball and place it outside of yourself on the left. Distinguish the difference between you and the red ball (your circumstance).

Notice you are separate from your circumstance. You are right here. Your circumstance is over there. Now, grow yourself ten times bigger than your circumstance. Now, grow yourself 20, 50, 100 times bigger than that measly, little circumstance.

What does that feel like? With this new visual, what idea, strategy, or call to action comes to mind? What will you act on right now as you see yourself 100 times bigger than your circumstance? Write it down. Move into that action step now.

*Mind Game #2:*

Take the lesson from Mind Game #1 and expand it. Again, picture your circumstance as a red ball and place it outside of yourself on the left. Distinguish the difference between you and the red ball (your circumstance). You are not financial struggle, illness, divorce, or rejection. If you are not your circumstances, who are you? If that challenge was not in your life, who would you be? Don't allow your circumstance to identify you. You decide who you are.

*Mind Game #3:*

Rewrite your story. Make it up. Redo the script. Go back in time and rewrite history. The subconscious mind doesn't know the difference between a made up story and the real version. Give yourself permission to rewrite your experiences of rejection, not fitting in, not being enough, or any story of lack and limitation.

What did you really want to have happen with that experience of rejection? Recall the circumstance and rewrite it.

How did you want your parent or guardian to show up for you? Rewrite it!

What did you really want to occur with that failure? Rewrite it!

What could have happened that would have created a greater sense of confidence instead of insecurity? Rewrite it!

The power in rewriting your history is you begin to neutralize the drama you've attached to these stories. You'll begin to loosen the grip these circumstances have on you. You may begin to realize where they were helpful for your growth. Your circumstances inspired you to be bolder, smarter, kinder, and more committed to your personal growth.

### Mind Game #4:

Craft an empowering vision. Create a script of what you want your future to look like. Actually write out your "Day in the Life of" manuscript. Then watch it in your imagination every day.

With the movie of your ideal future, you give your subconscious mind a command to fulfill.

Make no mistake; you already have a vision you are living into right now. But for most people, it is a negative vision or more of the same. This is crazy. Think about it; you would never go see a bad movie twice, right? Yet you do that every time you watch a "bad movie" of your past—a movie of when you failed or got rejected or experienced pain. Stop watching those negative movies! Press the imaginary eject button and replace the movie with an exciting, more empowering version of your life.

Remember, the subconscious mind cannot tell the difference between an imagined vision and a real one. You have great power in your imagination. Use it!

One of my favorite quotes by Albert Einstein is, "Imagination is more powerful than intellect."

Here is an example of how one of my clients used the power of her imagination to win a $10,000 cash prize!

Colleen wanted to win a $10,000 contest give-away her company was having at their next convention. Months before the event, she researched the details of the venue, the speakers, even the meeting room, She bought the suit she would wear. Then she wrote out the following vision and read it every day...

## Colleen's Empowering Vision

I pop out of bed like a piece of toast. I finally get to wear the Prada black suit I bought months ago that I hung outside my closet to look at everyday in anticipation of this moment. Today is the day we win the $10,000 cash prize.

We walk into the Bayshore Room and step on the bright, multi-colored carpet. I stop for a moment to take it all in. The beautiful punch-bowl chandeliers look like they are floating above me. The purple, green, and blue laser lights highlight the stage where we will win the $10,000. The aroma from the exotic flower arrangements makes me smile as I realize the scent is from my favorite flower, jasmine. We walk up to the front row and take our seats. The music and lights dim, signaling it's time to begin. Richard and Janine walk on stage. I notice the sparkling dollar sign pin on Janine's lapel and know that's a sign. She welcomes everyone and says, "Who's ready to win some money?"

The excited crowd cheers wildly. I feel my chair vibrate from the collective energy. Then, as if on cue, the audience falls silent. The music stops. All that can be heard is the sound of the tickets twirling around in the bin.

In my head I begin saying, "Colleen and John Riddle, Colleen and John Riddle, Colleen and John Riddle." I'm sending strong vibes in the direction of the stage. My heart seems to beat louder and louder. I look at John, sitting by my side and I smile. "It's our turn." He smiles and squeezes my hand.

Richard reaches into the bin with one hand and mixes up the tickets. With his other hand he reaches inside his suit jacket in search of his reading glasses, which he puts on. He pulls out a ticket, stares at it for a moment, then laughs and turns the ticket right side up, He smiles and glances at us sitting in the front row.

"And the winner of the $10,000 cash prize is…Colleen and John Riddle!"

John picks me up and spins me around. We sprint up on stage like a couple of contestants on *The Price Is Right*. We throw our arms around Richard and hug him. Richard turns us around to the screaming crowd.

We look across the room and see all of our leaders on their feet cheering for us. Richard tells us to put out our hand and begins counting…

"One hundred, two hundred, three hundred…" all the way to $10,000.

This movie script was written by Colleen several months before the event. Colleen and John shared with me that they watched that vision like a movie every day. The vision did become reality. Colleen told me later that nearly every detail of the movie script happened. The only surprise was the reality of the cash hitting her hand and how it took her breath away.

Here's the "Day in the Life of" manuscript that I wrote out five years ago and experience most of it as my reality today.

"Day in the Life of Lisa Jimenez"

I get up when I feel like it and walk out on our balcony to admire our beautiful water view. I smile as I breathe in the intense aromas of the flower gardens on our property. This is the fabulous waterfront home I've always wanted, its unique and beautiful decor representing our world travels and overflowing with so much love and tranquility.

My beloved brings me my coffee just the way I like it, along with a report of our sales that came in last night. I love passive income! We snuggle together and laugh as we share how grateful we are for each other and the life we have created. I look at him as he's talking, and I am moved with so much love and respect for him.

"You are such a good man. I love you," I say as I lean over to kiss him.

"I adore you," he whispers back to me. We smile and talk about the house-warming party we threw the weekend before, sharing stories about our wonderful kids, family, and friends who had so much fun enjoying delicious food, great wines, laughs, and stimulating conversation...until way past two in the morning. The party was pure pleasure to host as our staff is so competent and efficient.

I decide to go for a run and do my prayers and meditation on my pristine beach. I feel strong and fit as I run. My 117-pound body is in perfect rhythm with the ocean's waves. I presence my blessings and prayer requests and speak them out loud as a prayer of gratitude to God and to Jesus the Christ, whom I love so much.

As I return to the house, I find my beloved, who has just finished his workout, enjoying the delicious breakfast our chef has prepared for us. We eat together and talk about our upcoming world tour. We plan to launch it in Bali with a Mastermind retreat for our top Leaders. I picture their faces as they open their gifts and enjoy all the exotic excursions and special events we have planned for them.

From Bali, my beloved flies to Fiji for a big project he landed, and I jet off to Europe! We're always texting each other love notes on Viber and Skype and video on Periscope. We are an international couple.

Our company, Rx-Success, partners with an investor and receives a seven-figure publishing contract for the *Slay the Dragon* book series and movie. I marvel at the ease of collaboration we develop in our partnership. Many lives are changed for the better from this book tour and movie project. I am grateful for my calling and the opportunity to make a difference through my best-selling books, movies, and international speaking tours.

The final visit on my tour is in Africa where I reunite with my beloved for a week at the orphanage with the Unstoppable Foundation. We are thankful and humbled to have raised over $250,000 to help create more than a thousand villages for these beautiful souls of Africa. I can't wait to play kickball with these kids, read stories to them, and spend time loving on them and their families.

As my beloved and I relax in our first class seats on our way to Bali, he makes a toast. "To us and the privilege of being in love with each other and with our adventurous life!" He kisses me as our champagne glasses touch. The twinkle in my eyes and the smile on my face reflect the appreciation that beams in my heart.

Do you notice in my vision I include all the areas of life that make it juicy? Spirituality, relationships, love, health, career, finances, and contribution are all present in this vision. I include the five senses and pepper it with emotion and feelings that are authentic to me.

Now, it's your turn. First, make a list of goals in each of the areas of life that really matter to you. What do you really want to create in each of these areas in the next five years?

Spirituality:

Health:

Love/Relationships:

Family:

Career:

Finances:

Contribution:

From this list begin writing (in the present tense) what occurs for you on this day in the future and add emotion and feeling to it. Begin your movie script with "I wake up…" Be willing to write several drafts as you get clearer and clearer about what you really want. Push yourself in your beliefs about your core desires. Don't settle. Give yourself permission to go all out in your imagination. You are creating a future that will call you into action!

If you are willing to meditate over this vision every day and feel all the juicy emotions as if the vision is really happening, you will transform your subconscious mind. When your subconscious mind is aligned with this vision, your success is inevitable. Please email your "Day in the Life" movie script to me. It will be great to help you manifest it. Email to: Lisa@Rx-Success.com

There is great power in these Mind Games. They will literally change your life by changing the programming of your subconscious mind. *Success is created in the mind first.*

Review your answers to these mind games every morning for 30 days.

Change the meaning you give your circumstance.
Create a distinction between who you are and your circumstance. Grow yourself 100 times larger than your circumstance.
Rewrite your story of the past.
Craft a vivid and empowering vision of your future. Write out who you are being in this vision and what you are feeling. Allow yourself to become that person more and more every day.

Thoughts are things. Your predominant thoughts of today create your life experience tomorrow. Discipline yourself to think empowering thoughts. Practice imagining your dream life. See yourself confident, empowered, and effective. Give yourself permission to think the best, to dream the best, and you will live the best version of yourself. Everything is created twice. First in the mind, then in the physical realm.

## Dragon #2: *The Dragon of Circumstances*

**THE SWORD:** Perception

**THE PROCESS:** Utilize your perception to change the meaning you give your circumstances. Create a distinction between you and your circumstances and grow yourself bigger than them. Tap into the power of your imagination to rewrite your story and create an empowering vision to live into.

**THE RESULT:** You release all resistance that once held you back and are called to action by a compelling vision of your inspiring future.

**The Dragon Slayer Formula:** Hold the vision of what you want and do the inner work to reprogram your subconscious mind to align with that vision.

You are becoming a Dragon Slayer! With your empowering self-view, you know how to slay the Dragon of Circumstances. In the next chapter, we will move into slaying Dragon #3: The Dragon of Fear.

# Chapter 4:

## *How to Slay Dragon #3: The Dragon of Fear*

Fear is such an insidious Dragon. I wrote a whole book about it called, *Conquer Fear!* which has been published in seven languages. From that book and all the comments from readers, the truth about the Dragon of Fear remains the same:

It's not the fear that holds you back. *It's your relationship to fear that is the core problem.*

If you're like most people, you see fear as a reason to quit or as a sign that you're doing something wrong. You make fear mean you aren't good enough or strong enough. You allow fear to make you feel inferior.

Marketing slogans tout "No Fear!" Those companies are selling fear as a problem they've eradicated for you. You have been brainwashed to think having fear is bad or means you are weak. You keep yourself small and remain unfulfilled because of fear. You'd rather look good than take a risk. You'd rather face only what you can handle than get messy, let it rip, and do something so far out of your comfort zone, *even the bravest part of you is afraid!*

For me that was scuba diving. Even though I had travelled all over the world—mostly by myself—submerging myself under water with a tank of air petrified me. One time, on a cruise, I decided to give it a try. I boldly took the first class only to quit after the first dive—in a pool—because I had so much anxiety about being under water. As soon as the instructor put the regulator in my mouth, I panicked. I got myself out of the pool and dropped out of the class.

One night a dear friend said to me, "Lisa, I'm surprised that you don't scuba dive. You've traveled all over the world, but you're missing out on over seventy percent of what this world offers." Before I could respond, she added, "And do you know why you're missing out?"

I knew my line. "No, but I'm sure you're going to tell me."

"You're missing out on this underworld adventure because you're not willing to go through the discomfort of a learning curve."

She was right. I was keeping myself from a breakthrough because I wasn't willing to look dumb, get messy, feel embarrassed, and break through my insecurities. I just couldn't take the plunge.

Several years after my scuba dive failure, my boyfriend invited me to go sailing with him in the British Virgin Isles and—you guessed it—go scuba diving with him. There it was again—an instant panic attack. Only this time, equipped with my friend's comments on how I was missing out on over seventy percent of the world's beauty, I took another crack at the class.

Day one was not so good. I had several panic attacks in the water. But this time I stayed in the water! That was a quantum leap. I didn't enjoy that first lesson or the second. The entire time I felt embarrassed that a grown woman had so much fear; and insecurities about being under the water. It was messy. But, by being willing to be uncomfortable and let go of looking good, I knew I would eventually learn this new skill; so I did my best to relax and surrender to the process.

By the third lesson, which was an ocean dive, breathing with the regulator was second nature to me. My brain had reprogrammed itself. It was surprising to me how quickly this learning curve occurred. All the anxiety, apprehension, and even panic attacks were all worth it! That first experience of swimming with the fish in the underworld of the ocean was one of the most exciting adventures of my life.

Every person who has ever created or experienced something extraordinary has fear. The only difference between the successful person and the one who lives in mediocrity is the successful person *sees fear as a normal part of living a big life and they are willing to transform it.*

What about you? Where in your life do you step back because you allow fear to make you feel inferior? Are you more committed to looking good than you are to breaking through?

What are you facing right now that brings up the most fear?

_____

_____

Now, picture how you could expand that activity to bring up even more fear. Keep expanding the action step to intensify the level of fear.

Write down what you notice:

_____

_____

Finally, notice your resistance to even writing down your fear in the safety of your own home (or wherever you're reading this.) This is the subconscious mind doing its job to keep you from changing. To slay the Dragon of Fear, you need to be willing to look messy, feel uncomfortable, and let go of your addiction of looking good!

### Boldness Gets Rewarded

Knowing that fear is a part of every juicy experience I've ever had, I befriended my feelings of fear as I walked across the dance floor at the National Speaker's Association Gala event. Bob Proctor sat on the other side of the dance floor, and my plan was to ask him to write an endorsement for my upcoming book, *Conquer Fear!,* as we were dancing.

Surrounded by well-known speakers, authors, and thought leaders, I asked him my question. "Would you like to dance?" He responded, "No thank you."

I stood there paralyzed as my face turned deep red and thought to myself, "No thank you? What do I do now? Think, Lisa. Say something witty." But nothing witty or smart came to me. So I just smiled and said, "Oh, okay."

The walk of shame back to the other side of the dance floor was torture.

The next day, on my flight back home, I decided to write Bob Proctor a letter. The heading read, "You said no to me once..." The body of the letter was a request for him to write the endorsement for my book, *Conquer Fear!* I included a few chapters of the book and sent it off to him.

A few weeks later, my phone rang. Not recognizing the number, I almost didn't answer. But when I did I heard a familiar voice and chuckle on the other end of the phone. "Lisa Jimenez, this is Bob Proctor. I got your letter and request and I'm impressed," he began. "If there's anyone I would write an endorsement for a book with the title, *Conquer Fear!*, it's you!"

He continued to share with me his desire to help me. Not only did he write a stellar endorsement, he placed a book order of 100 copies for his team!

Over the next several years, Bob Proctor and his team gave me several opportunities to share my message as a speaker at their public seminars, on the Bob Proctor Cruises, and as a special guest on many training calls, blog posts, and podcast interviews.

But that's not the end of the story...

I was on the platform at a Vic Johnson *Claim Your Power* event. I had just finished sharing the "Will you dance with me?" story as the closing of my keynote speech. All of a sudden music started to play. The spotlight came back on the stage. And Bob Proctor walked toward me.

"Would you like to dance?" he asked me with a sweet, crooked grin on his face. We danced together as the entire crowd applauded, shouted, and shared the moment with us.

That moment, and all the blessings before, would never have happened if I wasn't willing to befriend my fear; *even after being rejected!* Fear is your green light to go. It is your opportunity to move into something bigger and more extraordinary than you could ever imagine. Boldness gets rewarded!

What about you? Will you befriend your fear and allow it to be your access to something more? The most effective way to do that is to cultivate your faith.

### *The Opposite of Fear Is Faith*

Unlike the famous slogan of "No fear," there are 365 verses in Scripture that say, "Fear not." Those words, "Fear not," imply there is fear but the command is not to let it stop you.

I remember one time in church the pastor suddenly asked the congregation, "How do you spell faith?" Everyone was silently thinking of a creative response.

"R-I-S-K!" he shouted. "When you feel fear, jump up and do something. Step out and say something. Your act of courage cultivates your faith and conquers your fear."

Even the smallest action step, taken in faith, will slay the Dragon of Fear, because one step of faith builds the courage to take another step and another.

Think of faith as a muscle. Faith needs to be worked out and strengthened to show the greatest results. And, just like working out a muscle, it may hurt a bit at first. But then the muscle gets stronger, the acts of valor get easier and faith strengthens. All it takes to build up to this level of strength and power is a mustard seed of faith. The mustard seed is the smallest of seeds and grows into one of the largest tree of its kind.

Fear can be your access to the miraculous side of life. It is often fear that causes you to go to God, tap into a higher power, seek Universal Laws, and expand beyond your own human capability.

**"Faith is more important than food."**
That was the headline in an article in *Psychology Today* where researchers shared the results of a study done in hospitals. Science shows us that healing occurs when faith is present. Neurologists have done countless studies explaining how the brain works and responds to thoughts of healing through acts of faith.
Cultivating your faith creates higher levels of achievement in business as well.
Polly's Story
Polly saw herself as a reluctant leader. Her biggest fear was making a mistake and letting others down. When her team asked her to attend their company's leadership retreat and come back to teach them what she learned, she said no. Well, she didn't say the word no. What she said was "The registration fee is too expensive."
When her team pulled together the finances for her to attend, their act of faith in her transformed her fear. She attended the leadership retreat and transformed into the leader her team knew she was.

When you cultivate your faith in who you will become and the impact you will have on yourself and others, you slay the Dragon of Fear.
Identify how transforming your fear and cultivating your faith will make a difference in your life and the lives of others.

_____

_____

_____

Give yourself permission to focus on the contribution you will be when you slay the Dragon of Fear. Train your brain to realize fear is normal. Fear means you're up to big things and is your green light to go. Fear can be the gift that leads you to access greater levels of faith and the miraculous side of life; the part of life that will surprise and delight you beyond what you can think or imagine.

## Dragon #3: *The Dragon of Fear*

**THE SWORD:** Faith

**THE PROCESS:** Befriend your fear by seeing it as a normal part of living a big life. Create a healthy relationship with fear by allowing fear to lead you to faith.

**THE RESULT:** Cultivating faith will make you unstoppable and give you access to a miraculous side of life.

**The Dragon Slayer Formula:** Hold the vision of what you want and do the inner work to reprogram your subconscious mind to align with that vision.

You've created an empowering self-view, created a new perspective of circumstances, and you cultivated your faith. In the next chapter, you'll learn how to slay Dragon #4: The Dragon of Ambiguity.

# Chapter 5:

## *How to Slay Dragon #4: The Dragon of Ambiguity*

Have you ever set a goal or made a decision and then something or someone made you change your mind?

Changing your mind is your prerogative; but when it becomes a pattern, it's a problem. This pattern of indecision is self-sabotage. Do any of these behaviors sound familiar?

You make a decision and then question your choice.

You say you want something and then decide you don't.

You sign up for an opportunity but never get started.

You have an idea that you're committed to, but then a "better one" captures your attention.

You jump in with all your heart, then allow someone's opinion to stop you.

These self-sabotage behaviors are the Dragon of Ambiguity. Remember, in Chapter 1 you learned your subconscious has one job to do: to keep you safe. And safe to the subconscious means "stay the same." The Dragon of Ambiguity will cause you to change your mind, judge your results, and question your ability in order to stop you from growing (changing).

Where is the Dragon of Ambiguity showing up in your life?

_____

_____

What decision or goal did you make that you are allowing other people's opinions to cause you to question that decision?

_____

_____

Where have you wimped out, given up, or lowered your expectation?

_____

_____

Most likely, the business, marriage, or school that you are presently in is your opportunity to master your mind and transform the way you think. Don't quit. You have been given an opportunity to slay the Dragon of Ambiguity right where you are.

## Three Causes of Ambiguity

### 1) Lack of Authenticity

If you set goals that are not aligned with your core values, all your results must come from will power. You learned in Chapters 1 and 2 that your will power can get results, but not for long. Sooner rather than later you'll get burned out or bored and you'll quit. However, you won't say you're quitting. You will continue to state your goals and say you are working toward them. But the Dragon of Ambiguity is behind those actions and it's just a matter of time before you sabotage your success. You will change your mind, shift your focus, or allow someone else's comments to take you out of the game.

It doesn't have to be that way...

You can slay the Dragon of Ambiguity when you put the force of your core values to work for you

### *Your Subconscious Mind Has Its Own Set of Values*

The most effective way to identify your subconscious' core values is to notice the people you most respect. What about their character and their lifestyle do you most admire? Is it their sense of humor? Power? Freedom? Integrity? Love? Is it their leadership ability? Influence? Intelligence? Wisdom? Do they have security? Wealth? Abundance? Family?

You respect and admire the character traits and the lifestyle they live because their character and lifestyle represents what really matters to you.

Your conscious mind wants to write the core values that "look good." But your subconscious mind is not concerned with looking good. That is why noticing what you admire in others reveals a more effective way to discovering your authentic core values.

Think of five people you most admire and make a list of why you admire them:

*Person #1:* _____

What About Them Do You Admire?

_____
_____
_____
_____

*Person #2:* _____

What About Them Do You Admire?

_____
_____
_____

*Person #3:* _____

What About Them Do You Admire?

_____
_____
_____

*Person #4:* _____

What About Them Do You Admire?

_____
_____
_____

*Person #5:* _____

What About Them Do You Admire?

_____
_____
_____

Look at the five reasons why you admire those people and you are looking at your core values.

One of the people I most admire is Lucille Ball. Lucy was funny and had a true boldness about her. She was willing to be outrageous with her humor and sense of silliness. Another quality Lucille Ball had was entrepreneurism. She created history; being the first actor to create wealth by asking for residuals when her show, *I Love Lucy!*, went into syndication.

Just from that story you can identify some of my core values, which are: a sense of humor, fun, innovation, boldness, freedom, and wealth.

The core values you hold in your subconscious mind are the driving force behind your behaviors. So, put them to work for you! Make a list of all the action steps you must follow to accomplish your goals and match them with your core values.

| "Must Do" Action Steps to Achieve My Goals and Dreams | How This Action Step Aligns With My Core Values |
|---|---|
| _____ | _____ |
| _____ | _____ |
| _____ | _____ |
| _____ | _____ |
| _____ | _____ |

When you keep your focus on what you get to do and how your core values are expressed in creating success, you will slay the Dragon of Ambiguity and enjoy the process of achievement.

## 2) Unmanaged Expectations
It's common for entrepreneurs to think their efforts will yield results faster than they really do. If you have a certain expectation of when results should come, the Dragon of Ambiguity will exhaust you as you are focused on something you don't have control over.

Manage your expectations by shifting your focus from results to activity.

Create specific goals around what you will do instead of what others need to do on a daily basis. Keep track of your daily action plan and shift your focus from being result-oriented to action-oriented. When you focus only on your daily activity, the results take care of themselves.

In health and fitness, it may be to walk, run, or move your body every day for at least ten minutes; to eat clean and healthy meals because eating healthy is who you are; to do 22 pushups every night before you go to bed.

In marriage and an intimate relationship, it may be to have a date night once a week, a hand-written card or message on the mirror once a week, and a daily "I love you."

In prospecting, it could be to invite two people every day to just take a look at your product, service or opportunity.

In personal development, it may be to meditate daily, read your vision statement, "Day in the Life of" (that you wrote in Chapter 3), and feel the inspiration that vision brings. Read a self-help book for 15 minutes everyday.

In spiritual development, it may be to pray before every meal or every night. It may be to declare a mantra or a statement of gratitude every time the phone rings.

In career, it may be to take a class in your field once a month and review the notes you took at that class every Sunday night.

In finance, it may be to save ten percent of your income or create a budget and clearly itemize where every dime goes.

These small, simple action steps can create massive results over time. Train your brain to focus only on the activity you do and watch how you improve your belief in the inevitable results that come. These action steps are enough. Small changes add up and multiply to create profound results. List some of the habits and disciplines you will put into your day—every day.

_____

_____

_____

### 3) Impending Boredom

Most entrepreneurs are incredibly creative and innovative. We all know those qualities are important in creating the business plan and strategic approach. So, you might be good at coming up with ideas and expanding those ideas. But innovation and creativity can keep you from actually "doing the business."

Success comes from following a proven system over and over again. This can be boring. An innovator who loves to try different things must guard against the inevitable boredom that seeps in from following a system.

One game I play that makes following the system fun is posting a chart in my office with a specific number of new prospects I add daily. I make it a game to fill in the spaces with the names of new people in my pipeline. I post a picture of a gift I'll treat myself to at the end of each month when I fill in all the spaces. Rewarding myself for my daily behavior instead of my results has empowered me to focus on only what I have control over.

The intention is to stay focused long enough for momentum to occur. It's like pumping water from a well. You pump the lever for a while with no results. You keep pumping even though you don't see water coming out of the spout. The water is rising but you can't see the results of your consistency because the well is under the ground. You keep pumping and pretty soon the water rises high enough for you to see the results of your consistent efforts.

## *The Power of Focus*

When you focus on an activity long enough, you create momentum. Momentum is that sweet spot where you and your activity get into a flow. Results come with ease. Your efforts duplicate and positive results are inevitable. All you have to do is focus long enough and momentum finds you every time.

Look back over the past one to three years and ask yourself, "What have I accomplished?" (Make a mental note of the accomplishments that come to mind.) Now ask yourself, "What could I have accomplished by being more intentional?"

Just imagine the implications of this. If you could have focused your mind even just two percent more of the time, where would you be today?

Now, move forward with intention. Drive your thoughts. Train your brain. Demand your success.

Harness the power of your mind with a daily practice of meditation and visualization.

Harness the power of your thoughts; eliminate a negative self-view by replacing it with a characteristic of who you want to become.

Harness the power of your words and speak words that create exactly what you want.

Harness the power of your emotions and notice when you feel good. Give yourself permission to really "milk" that feeling of exuberance!

Harness the power of momentum with "a daily activity" that compounds over time.

### *The Power of Intention*

Today is going to be a great day. How do I know that? I know it will be a great day, because I said so! My intention is to have a great day and that intention creates the context I'm living within.

When you set an intention, you are harnessing great power in your mind. Your intention creates a context for your subconscious to live from and your behaviors actually mirror that intention. That's power!

You harness this power with your words and the intent behind your words. Your meekness is not helping. You need to slay the Dragon of Ambiguity and stop wimping out by being a victim or having the belief you can't have what you want. Decide what you want. Speak it. Declare it. Realize your words and the intent behind them will manifest...because you said so.
Jason, one of my high-level coaching clients, shared a specific challenge he was dealing with that week.

"What exactly do you want to occur from this challenge?" I asked him and then added for clarity, "What is the intention you have for your leaders and your company from this challenge?"

Without hesitation he said, "My intention is to have my leaders gain a higher level of integrity and for the culture of my company to be greatly enhanced." I repeated his intention and added, "And that is what will occur."

"You are an eternal optimist, Lisa." he replied.

"I'm not only an eternal optimist, Jason," I replied. "I am a creator and what I say will happen. Your leaders will gain a greater level of integrity and greatly enhance the morale and culture of your company, because we said so."

I completed the coaching call with his assignment: "Share your intention with your leaders from the context that you are a man who believes the intention will happen, because you said so."

Just imagine what your life will look like one year from now when you harness the power of focus and intention. You are "being" the person who lives your dream life. And that way of being creates the posture you need to remain self-motivated long enough to experience momentum.

## *The Power of the Brain*

You have all you need to slay the Dragon of Ambiguity. You just need to be willing to access a pea-size group of cells in the lower part of your brain called the Reticular Activating System (RAS). The RAS is located in the stem of your brain and works as a phenomenal filtering system. This is like a gatekeeper that allows only certain stimuli to get into your conscious awareness. In every moment there are over two million bits of sensory information bombarding your data system. Can you image what life would be like if you were aware of all these bits of information? You would go insane. So, you have a reticular activating system to help you filter all this stimulation. In fact, the RAS lets in and processes about 11 bits of information in any given moment.

So, I've got a question for you...
What do you think decides which 11 bits of information get past the gatekeeper (the RAS)?

The answer is: It's your most active and focused thoughts. It's what you think about most of the time. You actually train your brain what to see and experience in the world.

This is profound. Just imagine the implications of this. You can actually train your brain to see solutions instead of problems, love instead of hate, growth instead of destruction, and goodness instead of evil. In each of those examples, both of the extremes exist, but you train your brain (your RAS) to notice one; and then it will filter out the other.

You've most likely experienced your RAS after you purchased a car. All of a sudden, you begin noticing all the identical cars to yours. Through the RAS you see what matches your most common thoughts. This explains why you notice certain things in life, while your friend—someone you're close to and with whom share many interests—notices entirely different things.
You can train the RAS what to notice.

This takes a discipline on your part to train your conscious mind to hold images of what you want. See your goals realized. Create a clear picture of what you want to attract. Set the intention of what you want to see and notice today.
Demand it. Tell your brain what to think. Lead your imagination to picture the beauty and contribution of your goals being realized. Drive your success by driving your RAS.
Test the power of your RAS today. Decide what you're going to focus on. Let's say it's a butterfly. See the image of the butterfly in your mind over and over again. Feel how excited you're going to be when you see it. Focus on that image of the butterfly. Continue to focus on the butterfly in your mind and watch how your RAS, like radar, begins noticing all the butterflies.

Realize the butterflies were always there, but by focusing on that image in your mind, your RAS did what the RAS is designed to do and, just like radar, the RAS identified the butterflies and filtered out everything else.

Everything is created twice. First in the mind then in the physical realm.

The reticular activating system can also transform your behaviors. When you hold the image of you being bold, productive, kind, and smart; you train your RAS to attract the opportunities to become this person. Create clarity in who you want to be, and you will become a person who is courageous instead of fearful; faith-filled instead of fear-based; decisive instead of apprehensive.

The brain thinks in pictures, not words. So picture what you want. Picture yourself being courageous, powerful, expansive, kind, and confident. Picture the things, circumstances, and results you want and you will train your brain to begin noticing them. Intend it. Demand it.

"Whatever is true, whatever is honorable, whatever is just, whatever is pure, whatever is lovely, whatever is commendable, if there is any excellence, if there is anything worthy of praise, think about these things." Philippians 4:8

**WARNING:** Remember, the language of manifestation is emotions.

You could be thinking about the car you want or a new level to achieve in your company and it brings up feelings of lack. Thoughts about attracting the love of your life could generate feelings of pain. Thinking about boatloads of cash could bring up feelings of unworthiness. You must be sure the thoughts you are disciplining your mind to have create feelings that empower you.

Your thoughts cause your RAS to attract their match and your FEELINGS give you the power to ACT on the things you are attracting. This combination of the head and heart helps create the alignment you need in your conscious and subconscious minds.

### Dragon #4: The Dragon of Ambiguity

**THE SWORD:** Intention

**THE PROCESS:** You have great power in your ability to intend. Make a choice. Decide what you want and state that intention. Be unattached to how you will accomplish your intention; just be very attached to your commitment to create the intention.

**THE RESULT:** When you state an intention, you create the posture, mindset, and alignment to attract it. You train the brain with the RAS to notice the people, ideas, and opportunities you need to accomplish that intention; and filter out everything else.

**The Dragon Slayer Formula:** Hold the vision of what you want and do the inner work to reprogram your subconscious mind to align with that vision.

You've tapped into the most powerful force available. Your spoken word and the intention behind it will give you the fuel you need to stay committed to the process of achievement. In the next chapter, you'll learn how to slay Dragon #5: The Dragon of Efforting.

# Chapter 6:

## *How to Slay Dragon #5: The Dragon of Efforting*

The Dragon of Efforting represents a form of sabotage that keeps you addicted to the effort of achievement.

Let's face it, you get accolades from working hard; you get respect from overcoming; you feel valued from being busy.
My client, Carrie, sat across from me at a coffee shop. She reported that all her activity goals were met and she had just enjoyed one of her best weeks in business. And yet...something was missing.
She dropped eye contact from me and focused on the placemat. "I don't feel like I did enough," she said, her voice suddenly very small.
"Carrie, that's just self-sabotage," I replied and explained how the subconscious is wired at "never enough." It values "busyness" and drama over consistency and peace.
At that exact moment a man rushed in with his cell phone up to his ear. You could tell he was agitated by the long line he had to stand in and continued to check his watch and talk on the phone until it was his turn to order. He was busy.
"Gosh...on his phone, checking his watch, obviously in a hurry. He must be really successful!" I joked.
Carrie laughed. "I think I get it!" she said with a smile.
What about you? Are you like Carrie and feel you always have to be doing more to deserve success?
Slaying the Dragon of Efforting is about doing less to have more.

This is counterintuitive to everything you've been taught about achievement. But it is your access to another level of inner power and ultimately a greater level of success.

When you adopt the mindset of doing less to have more, you give yourself permission to:

1. Delegate:  Ask for help and assign others the tasks you're not good at or don't want to do.
2. Duplicate Yourself and Your Content:  Mentor others to create residual income. Create books, audio programs, podcasts, and other resources. Lease the rights to your intellectual content. Create multiple sources of income. Access geometric growth and the power of duplication.

These ideas give you greater access to the most powerful commodity you have: Your time—and duplicating that time.

When you slay the Dragon of Efforting, you let go of your addiction to the effort of achievement. You release the need to be a "lone ranger" and allow other people to shine in their partnership with you.

The other great benefit of slaying the Dragon of Efforting is the spiritual power you gain access to.

On Fifth Avenue in midtown Manhattan, New York, you'll find two famous statues very close to each other. One of them, in front of the GE Building, is the bronze statue of the Greek god Atlas. A muscular Atlas strains to carry the cosmos on his shoulders. According to Greek mythology, this task was for him a curse rather than an act of courage. The other statue is found in Saint Patrick's Cathedral, just across the street from Atlas. It portrays Jesus as a young boy effortlessly holding the whole world in his hand. His hand seems designed to carry it.

Do less to have more means you stop striving and start trusting. You partner with a Force greater than yourself.

### *Your Guidance System*

One of the best examples of exactly what it looks like to do less and have more is a GPS. I'm sure you've used a navigational system in your car or a rental car to get directions to reach your destination. It works like this:

You punch in an address and the GPS calculates the best route to get you there.

What's the first thing you need to do before the GPS can give you the route?

You need to know where you want to go.

As soon as you punch in the address, the GPS calculates the best route for you to take. Every detail is calculated for you. All you need to do is be willing to follow. You can't argue with what the GPS tells you. You can't question the given route. You can't believe it was so easy to come up with. You just follow.

I want you to notice something...

Does the GPS give you all of the directions at once? No, it doesn't. Even though the entire route is calculated, the GPS gives you only the first command. And, you don't get the second step until you complete on the first one. Your role is to trust the GPS and act on its directions, one command at a time.

But let's say you accidentally make a wrong turn. What does the GPS do now? Does it tell you to quit? Does it call you an idiot and yell at you that you messed up...again? Of course not; it simply recalculates.

It's the same with this Force inside of you. You have a clear goal of where you want to go and you ask for directions. The entire route is calculated for you, but you are given just one command at a time...and get the next command only when you complete the one before. And when you make a wrong turn, this Force calmly redirects you from where you are at. No going back to the beginning. You are always moving forward, divinely guided.
If you stay connected and keep following, reaching your goals is inevitable. The key is to stay connected. That's your part.

Remaining connected to your inner guidance system gives you access to the power of alignment, manifestation, and intuition:

## *The Power of Alignment*

The definition of alignment is: A position of agreement. Your job is to continue to stay in alignment with who you say you are and what you intend to create.

Most people who fly don't know that when they take a flight from LAX to JFK, the airplane will be off course more than it will be on course. Yet, that airplane lands exactly where the pilot wants it to land in JFK. The pilot's job is to keep bringing the airplane back on course every time it veers to the left or to the right. This is the description of your job as well. You are the pilot of your life. Even though you may be off course most of the time, you can still land where you want to land and accomplish what you want, when you continue—in every moment—to get yourself back on course. Do the work to be in alignment with your new self-view and the intentions you set for your day; every day and in every moment.

## The Power of Manifestation

When you master alignment, you have the power to manifest what you want. The definition of manifestation is: An event, action, or object that clearly shows or displays something.

The Force that I spoke of earlier wants to be shown, made known, and displayed. When you are aligned with this Force, you ask for something and it is given.

## The Power of Intuition

The definition of intuition is: The ability to understand something immediately, without the need for conscious reasoning.

When you are in agreement with this spiritual realm, you accomplish your goals with your inner gifts of intuition, insight, wisdom, and instinct. Intuition and insight is the ability to discern the true nature of a situation. You just know what to say and do. Your activity seems to be inspired. Wisdom is the ability to think and act using knowledge and experience. Instinct is a pattern of behavior that stems from an impulse. You feel a pulling toward your goal and it's natural for you to move forward.

Just imagine how bold you will become and how exciting achieving your goals will be when you are aligned with a Force greater than your intellect, guided by your intuition, and confident in the partnership of manifestation.

Anything...anything...ANYTHING is possible for you!
Your life is full of serendipity, coincidences, and the unexplainable. You're always at the right place at the right time. You feel abundant, blessed, and highly favored. I call it the realm of the miraculous. This is what your life will begin to look like:

You just happen to be standing in line at the coffee house and the gentleman behind you is talking about a great book he just read and it is your book. The connection is made and he hires you to speak at his next company event!
You are at a bookstore in San Francisco (3000 miles away from your home) and you overhear someone at the counter asking about a book she wants to buy and it's your book.
You come up with the perfect idea or solution and it seems to have been dropped out of the sky. It's exactly what you needed and you execute with velocity as everything just falls into place.
You have a publishing date for your book and you fail to make it...twice, only to realize that the third and final debut date just happens to be on September 11th, the same day of the 9/11 terrorist attack and your book is titled, *Conquer Fear!*
You're walking down the Champs Elysees in Paris and hear someone calling your name. You look up to discover one of your clients who just happens to be in Paris at the same time as you.

Your plane is delayed so you spend some time in the airport bookstore. You strike up a conversation about your book with a lady who just happens to be the buyer for the store.

These are just some real-world examples I have experienced. What about you? What have you experienced in your life that just seemed to be gifted to you? When did serendipity occur? What "out of the blue" idea came to you? How did the unexplainable happen in your life? Where have you experienced coincidences? Make a list of as many as you can remember. Notice. Read and reread what you wrote down.

_____

_____

_____

Throughout the entire book we've been talking about aligning your head and your heart (your conscious and subconscious minds). When you are aligned, you create harmony within. That's the goal of this message! The daily disciplines you learned in this book are a lifelong process. This process will continue to expand what's possible for you by evolving who you can become.

I believe this is the purpose of your life: To continue to expand what's possible and evolve yourself, become more, and enjoy the experience of that evolution.

**WARNING:** You may be resisting this teaching because it seems too easy or it's just too "out there" for you.

That's a form of self-sabotage. The Dragon of Efforting shows up as resistance to a message that sounds "too easy" or "too different from the norm."

In the latter 1930s, the Duff Company invented the cake mix. All the cook had to do was add water. It didn't sell. The housewife, and the purchasing public in general, wouldn't buy the product. They didn't trust it, because the directions were just too darn easy. The cake mix was taken off the shelves and the formula redesigned to add eggs, oil, and water. General Mills, Betty Crocker, and Pillsbury followed and created one of the most successful inventions in the food industry.

Richard Branson launched The Spaceship Company (TSC), a subsidiary of Virgin Galactic, in 2005. The company has contracts to develop commercial space ships and launch aircrafts for space travel. They will fly you to Sydney from Los Angeles in 20 minutes. In one of Sir Branson's interviews, he shared that the biggest challenge they will face: Changing the public's mindset around flying in a rocket.

One of the final exercise for you to do to slay the Dragon of Efforting is to notice resistance and transform it. Resistance shows up as an unconscious commitment to stay the same. Some unconscious commitments look like this:

I am more committed to comfort than change.
I am more committed to safety than to taking a risk.
I am more committed to routine than to trying something new.
I am more committed to being right than to growth.
I am more committed to drama than to peace.

Read the list of unconscious commitments again, only this time switch the words. Release resistance by creating new commitments.

I am more committed to change than to being comfortable.
I am more committed to taking a risk than to being safe.
I am more committed to try something new than to routine.
I am more committed to growth than to being right.
I am more committed to peace than drama.

You will know that you have no resistance to something when it manifests in your life. This is called alignment.

A Dragon Slayer creates alignment (agreement) in the following areas:

Goals and Beliefs

Thoughts and Feelings (Emotions)

Values and Actions

The Dragon Slayer's Formula to Achieving Goals

What specific goal do you want to achieve in the next year?
_____
_____
_____

Let's say you wrote down a weight loss goal of 45 pounds.

Under that goal write your current beliefs, thoughts, and emotions about losing that weight. You may have a belief you don't have time to work out. You lack the skill to know how to lose weight. You don't have the money to eat healthy. You have thoughts like "I've tried that before and it didn't work." Your emotions may have screamed, "Here we go again! I feel like a failure already."

Or you may have identified subconscious beliefs like:
What if I really did lose 45 pounds and I would have to
_____ (fill in the blank). That thought brings a lot of fear of the unknown!

The purpose of writing the limiting beliefs, thoughts, and emotions is so you can see the gap—the gap between who you are now and who you get to become! That's the whole reason manifesting is so good for you; it allows you to become even more. Evolving yourself and expanding what's possible is a big part of why you exist. It's not really about losing the weight, making more money, or advancing in a career; it's more about WHO YOU MUST BECOME to accomplish those things.

The next step is to make a list of the beliefs, thoughts, and emotions that support your core values (what truly matters to you) in your goal of losing 45 pounds (or whatever your goal was). WHY do you really want to lose 45 pounds?

_____

_____

_____

HOW will the process of attaining that goal make you a better person?

_____

_____

_____

WHAT will be the ultimate benefits and HOW will they be aligned with your core values (what really matters to you)? List the people who will be an inspiration to along the way.

_____

_____

_____

WHO do you need to become to let go of the weight and be more healthy?

_____

_____

_____

HOW will it feel to be 45 pounds lighter? How will it feel to be a person who accomplishes your goals? How will this benefit the people you care about? How is it good for the world?

_____
_____
_____

Really milk these juicy emotions. These are the feelings that will fuel your behaviors. Do this same exercise with all of your goals.

When you do the work to align your current beliefs, thoughts, emotions, and values with the future you, you'll watch how miracles appear, serendipity occurs, out-of-the-blue ideas come, coincidences happen, and the unexplainable becomes your everyday life experience.

I have done this same process with every goal I've manifested. I do the inner work—every day—to align my goals, beliefs, thoughts, feelings, and values. I actually transformed into the person my goal called me to be.

Your future YOU is calling you to become even better. This is the beautiful gift of accomplishing your goals. It's not just the prize, but the pride in who you become along the way.

When you "do the inner work" you are tapped into the amazing power of manifestation—partnering with God. I find that exhilarating. With our cooperation and partnership, God shows the miraculous through us. I'm not saying God or these forces of love and goodness don't exist without us. I'm saying that they are expressed through us. We are the "proof" of their existence.

It is God's very nature to manifest Himself in and through your life. Who knows? Maybe that's why we were created...just to experience God's nature in us and all that manifests from that partnership.

The natural mind cannot comprehend spiritual things to the depth of understanding given by the intuitive mind. Reason and rational thought are often useful after the fact and not before. But intuition is your access to the Mind and Heart of God, where you have a divine instinct about situations, people, and decisions.

I believe intuition is one of the most profound examples of how your are made in the image of God. The more time you allow for meditation and quieting the mind, the more your intuition is heightened. Life becomes magical. Experiences are intensified and a whole new level of living begins to occur.

Your willingness to sharpen your intuition will cause you to experience:

Perfect timing
Synchronicity
Divine knowledge
Rich blessing and favor
A blessing for others
A great sense of love and well-being

## Dragon #5: *The Dragon of Efforting*

**THE SWORD:** INTUITION

**THE PROCESS:** Daily rituals of prayer and meditation help you connect with a higher power. You quiet the mind to tap into your inner gifts of intuition, insight, instinct and wisdom. You release your need to control and open up new possibilities of collaboration and partnerships.

**THE RESULT:** When you quiet the mind, you tap into your inner powers and intellectual faculties of intuition, instinct, and wisdom. Serendipity occurs on a regular basis. You're always in the right place at the right time. You collaborate with ease and expand what's possible for you by duplicating yourself, and creating residual time and income. You do less and have more.

**The Dragon Slayer Formula:** Hold the vision of what you want and do the inner work to reprogram your subconscious mind to align with that vision.

You've created an empowering self-view. You've transformed the meaning you give your circumstances. You cultivate your faith and shift your focus to what you want to be, do, and have. You tap into the power of the spoken word with clear and powerful intentions. And you know how to quiet the mind and connect with your inner gifts of intuition, instinct, insight, and wisdom.

You are a Dragon Slayer! In the next and final chapter, you'll learn the Dragon Slayer's mission.

# Chapter 7:

## *You Are a Dragon Slayer!*

With every fresh goal you set, there will be a gap between who you are now and who your goal calls you to be.

The gap between aspiration and achievement is development. In achieving that goal, you get to become a new person. The process of that development is a privilege. You are meant to grow. Your life is supposed to evolve. That is the path of a Dragon Slayer.

### *The Mission of a Dragon Slayer*

Dragon Slayers are prophetic. They are able to see what is hidden behind the issues
they face. They know that everything serves. They take complete responsibility for the way they feel at all times; and if an emotional adjustment is needed, they cause it. They can focus their way back into feeling good without needing a problem or a personal flaw to be resolved. Dragon Slayers see the gifts in the people around them. They see goodness and opportunity with startling clarity. They have this power because they are aligned with the One who gives this power.

As a Dragon Slayer, you become who your best life demands you to be. You live
from the accomplishment of your goals and dreams. You have a posture that looks like you believe in the inevitability of those goals and dreams—all because you

understand that what you do matters. The goals and dreams you achieve are important as they are the impact you have the privilege to make on others. Most importantly...

Who you become and what you create is the gift you give to the world.

Your final assignment is to answer the following questions as a Dragon Slayer!

What do you really want?

_____

_____

_____

Who do you need to become in order to achieve it?

_____

_____

_____

What can you do today to begin aligning yourself with that "way of being"?

_____

_____

_____

Sit in the silence right now and listen to your first inspired action step. Act on it right now... And, just like with the GPS, the next step will be revealed. When you act on that inspired action you ignite the path of your goal being realized and you cultivate the inevitability of your dreams.

You will become the person who lives your dream life from the inside out. That truth is the intention of this book: To program your subconscious mind to align with the vision you have of your dream life.

Experiencing the life you really want is that simple. But make no mistake; it isn't easy. You've got to stay committed to doing the inner work you learned in *Slay the Dragon*. Master your mind and give yourself permission to be great.

Success is your birthright. Progress is your natural way of being. Expansion is how you were designed.


Richest blessings,

*Lisa*

Lisa Jimenez M.Ed.

## *A Dragon Slayer's Daily Mantras:*

## *Dragon #1: The Dragon of Limiting Self-View*

**THE SWORD:** WILL

I am a Dragon Slayer. I realize how my childhood nickname and the decisions I made when I was seven years old have affected my results and kept me small. I know I have the power to re-create myself by setting new expectations of who I say I am. I know how to discipline myself to live into my new and empowering
self-view.

## *Dragon #2: The Dragon of Circumstances*

**THE SWORD:** PERCEPTION

I no longer collapse who I am with my circumstances. I grow myself bigger than my circumstances and I am open to the ways I will overcome them. I know how to rewrite my story and I give myself permission to see my circumstances as empowering forces to ignite even more greatness from myself and from life. I have an empowering vision of the life I am creating and allow that vision to call me into action.

## *Dragon #3: The Dragon of Fear*

**THE SWORD:** FAITH

I accept fear as a natural part of growing and achieving my goals. I no longer give fear so much energy. I see it as my green light to go! I tap into my imagination and live my life from the vision of my goals and dreams already achieved. I cultivate my faith in a higher power and in the inevitability of my dreams.

## Dragon #4: The Dragon of Ambiguity

### THE SWORD: INTENTION

I create an intention every day. I cause my intention from the way I am being. I become the person my dream life calls me to be. I allow the power of my words, thoughts, and visions to move me into action. I attract the people, ideas, and opportunities I need to accomplish my goals one day at a time. I fall in love with the process of achievement and becoming the person my goals and dreams call me to be.

## Dragon #5: The Dragon of Efforting

### THE SWORD: INTUITION

I am aligned with a Force greater than me. I tap into my intuition and inner wisdom, and allow these gifts to guide me every day. My subconscious mind is aligned with my goals and dreams, and I am being the person who lives my dream life. Success comes to me with ease and I respond boldly. Serendipity, coincidence and the miraculous are a part of my daily experience. I let go of control and partner with other like-minded people. I have the belief that my success is inevitable and I enjoy the journey of who I am becoming along the way. I work less to have more.

# EPILOGUE

You have heard a recurring message throughout the entire *Slay the Dragon* book: The only thing holding you back from what you really want is you. When you do the inner work to reprogram your subconscious mind, success is inevitable.

Through the process of reprogramming your subconscious mind, you become the best version of you! Declare this life-changing mantra every day:
"I can have whatever I am willing to be."

Fall in love with the process of transforming yourself. Your willingness to do the inner work is the gift you give yourself and others. Your life experience and the impact that experience will have on others will be worth everything you went through to reprogram your subconscious mind and transform your life.

You have been called for such a time as this. It is no accident that you read this book and learned the process of becoming a Dragon Slayer. It's your time. The world needs you to step up, slay your Dragons, and get on with evolving into the best version of you!

# OTHER RESOURCES
*by Lisa Jimenez M.Ed.*

## *Conquer Fear!*

*A unique blend of psychology and theology to change your beliefs and results*

The biggest barrier that entrepreneurs have to overcome is fear. Fear of rejection. Fear of making decisions. Fear of change. Fear of failure. And of course the big one – fear of success! It is this fear (and all of its cousins like worry, anxiety, and self-doubt) that paralyzes you and keeps you from higher levels of success.

You will laugh (and be shocked) when you discover the hidden messages that your behavior is screaming out. Through personal stories and humor, Lisa reveals the most common ways a belief systems can actually repel success! Positive thinking by itself just isn't enough. This book will teach the steps to improve your results by cultivating your faith and developing an unstoppable belief system.

**In this powerful message, you will:**
Identify and overcome self-limiting beliefs;
Stop procrastination and self-sabotage;
Reject rejection with the L.O.A. (Law of Average);
Break through negative programming NOW;

The power in this book comes from blending the two disciplines of psychology and spirituality. By blending the head and heart aspects of motivation, you'll learn the process of breaking through fear and self-limiting beliefs to become more confident, bold, and adventurous in life!

# *Don't Mess With the Princess!*

*Don't Mess with the Princess!* is a provocative and thought-provoking book that will help you reclaim your power and stop settling for less that you are.  It's about breaking through harmful beliefs about being a powerful women in the boardroom and the bedroom. You'll be inspired to shift your beliefs about femininity and create the mind-set you need to prosper in your professional and personal life.

If You Have Ever:

- Sat by the phone waiting for it to ring;
- Undergone "Haagen-Dazs therapy" after a breakup;
- Wondered if you were good enough;
- Played small to fit in; or,
- Blamed your parents, kids, spouse, or crazy ex for not achieving your dreams... Then this book is for you!

Lisa's message will slap you in the face while it heals your heart. It will rock your world while it restores your power. And, it will shake your beliefs while it empowers your dreams!

*Don't Mess With the Princess!* reveals the truth about femininity and the power of being a woman in business and in life. It will inspire you to discover your ideal career, attract your dream mate, and manifest your dreams to live a life you love.

# SPEAKING PROGRAMS
*by Lisa Jimenez*

## *Slay the Dragon!*
## Keynote & Seminar

People who succeed in business and life are the people who have a "success mind-set." The reality is most people are wired to fail and that's why they sabotage their success. This program will change that. Lisa is an expert at teaching people how to retrain the brain and create the mind-set they need to succeed.

Through her proven system, Lisa teaches your people how to identify and slay the 5 Dragons of Self-Sabotage. They will learn how to master their mind, discipline their emotions, and train their subconscious to win!

### *Your people will learn how to:*
- Identify their values and tap into the power of integrity;
- Set clear goals and objectives that align with values;
- Access the power of the (RAS) Reticular Activating System to retrain the brain;
- Craft a compelling vision that inspires action;
- Recreate their self-view and transform perception;
- Turn setbacks into stepping stones; and,
- Create the mind of a game changer!

Every success is created twice. First, with a decision in the mind and then in the physical realm. Give your people a radical transformation and create success from the inside out. Through this empowering program, your people will become their own

Dragon Slayer ~ ready and equipped to slay the Dragons of Self-Sabotage!

A great program as a keynote or a full day advanced seminar.

# *Conquer Fear!*
# Keynote & Seminar

The biggest barrier that all distributors have to overcome is fear. Fear of rejection. Fear of failure. Fear of leadership. Fear of making decisions. And of course the big one - fear of success! It is fear (and all of its cousins like worry, anxiety, and self-doubt) that paralyzes your people, and keeps them from succeeding.

This program will give your sales force a practical action plan that will empower them to befriend their fear, reject rejection, and be free to get on with creating and achieving their goals! Lisa will guide them in an understanding of why they do what they do and help them break through self-sabotage behaviors.

Through personal stories and humor, Lisa reveals the most common ways that people's belief system can actually repel success! This program goes beyond positive thinking and teaches how to improve results by developing a powerful belief system.

### *Your people will learn how to:*

- Identify and overcome self-limiting beliefs;
- Stop procrastination and self-sabotage;
- Reject rejection with the L.O.A. (law of average);
- Raise their self-esteem and confidence level;
- Create momentum to stay motivated; and,
- Increase their bottom line by closing more sales.

A great program to kick off your convention with a bang!

# *Don't Mess with the Princess!*
# Keynote & Seminar

Let's face it, as far as women have come in business, there are still too few who are making top earnings. In this fun and thought-provoking message, Lisa will inspire your female leaders to break through limiting beliefs about femininity, power, and success.

Lisa uses humor to reveal the, "3 personality types in every woman" and teaches how to access each one for greater results. Whether it's the Queen who needs to control, or the Duchess who plays small to fit in, or the Princess who owns her power, your people will laugh out loud when they identify with each one. And they'll cry with joy when they learn how to break through them and give themselves permission to win!

### *Your people will learn how to:*

- Balance winning in business while maintaing a happy home life;
- Cultivate the power of their femininity to lead and inspire themselves and others;
- Manage their emotions and transform their results; and,
- Have more confidence and create a lasting impact for the company, community and the planet!

A great program to kick off or close out your convention!

# Rich Life Mastermind Retreat & Coaching Program

When was the last time you spent a day, a weekend—or a whole week thinking about your ideal life and strategizing a plan to achieve it? Research proves it's the people who visualize their goals, create a plan of action, and have support from others-- achieve what they want.

That's exactly what *The Rich Life Mastermind Retreats and Coaching Program* is designed to do. First, the power of the Mastermind will give you the structure and insight to develop your goal and plan of action. The coaching will give you the structure and accountability to remain in action. Finally, and most importantly, the luxury of the retreat itself will give you the prosperity mind-set you need to drive your behaviors, create momentum, and achieve your goals with ease!

For nine years, I've been taking entrepreneurs to exotic cities around the globe for their transformation at my Rich Life Mastermind Retreats. We've been to Paris, Maui, Prague, Sydney, Buenos Aires, Bangkok, Florence, Bali, Costa Rica and even a castle in Tuscany.

The mission is simple, yet profound: *Offer a total immersion experience of luxury, adventure, connection, possibility, and fun to **Radically Transform the Self-View, Retrain the Brain, and Create a Prosperity Mindset.***

## *The Rich Life Mastermind Retreat and Coaching Program will help you:*

- Break through limiting beliefs and blind spots that hold you back;
- Gain clarity in what you really want and a solid plan to achieve it;

- Remain motivated with weekly accountable calls; and,
- Create a prosperity mindset to take your business and life to a whole new level.

The Weekly Business Coaching coupled with a total emersion experience at the 5 Day Rich Life Mastermind Retreat is the most powerful combination available to retrain your brain, transform your mind-set, and drive your behaviors to achieve your goals and live your dream life. You will love who you become!

*Connect with Lisa!*

 www.rx-success.com

 http://www.facebook.com/lisajimenez1111

 http://twitter.com/richlifelisa

 http://twitter.com/richlifelisa

 https://www.youtube.com/user/RxSuccess